ALABASTER
GUIDED MEDITATIONS

JOHN

READ | REFLECT | RESPOND | REST

Guided Meditations by Jan Johnson

NLT.

ivp

An imprint of InterVarsity Press
Downers Grove, Illinois

InterVarsity Press
P.O. Box 1400, Downers Grove, IL 60515-1426
ivpress.com | email@ivpress.com

InterVarsity Press® is the book-publishing division of InterVarsity Christian
Fellowship/USA®, a movement of students and faculty active on campus
at hundreds of universities, colleges, and schools of nursing in the United
States of America, and a member movement of the International Fellowship
of Evangelical Students. For information about local and regional activities,
visit intervarsity.org.

All Scripture quotations are taken from the *Holy Bible*, New Living Translation,
copyright ©1996, 2004, 2015. Used by permission of Tyndale House
Publishers. All rights reserved.

New Living Translation, *NLT*, and the New Living Translation logo are
registered trademarks of Tyndale House Publishers.

ISBN 978-0-8308-4895-9 (print)
ISBN 978-0-8308-4896-6 (digital)

Printed in the United States of America ♾

Library of Congress Cataloging-in-Publication Data
A catalog record for this book is available from the Library of Congress.

P   13   12   11   10   9   8   7   6   5   4   3   2   1
Y   30   29   28   27   26   25   24   23   22   21   20

INTRODUCING ALABASTER GUIDED MEDITATIONS

In these pages you'll find an evocative pairing of photographs with the New Living Translation of the Bible. To deepen your experience of both Scripture and image, we've added guided meditations, written by experienced Bible teachers.

Lectio divina is a practice of Scripture reading, prayer, and meditation with a long and rich heritage in the Christian tradition. As early as the fourth century, the term *lectio divina* was being used by Christians like St. Ambrose, St. Hilary of Poitiers, and St. Augustine to refer to reading Scripture. The practice was developed over the years and formalized in the twelfth century— notably by St. John of the Cross, whose famous maxim says, "Seek in reading and you will find in meditation; knock in prayer and it will be opened to you in contemplation." These are the four traditional steps of lectio divina: reading, meditation, prayer, and contemplation. These steps are presented here as (1) Read, (2) Reflect, (3) Respond, and (4) Rest.

Lectio divina invites us into the Bible's world, prompting us to imagine the biblical scene, to feel what the writers of Scripture might have felt, and to listen for what the Holy Spirit might be prompting us to consider. Visio divina applies this process to images, inviting us into prayerful interaction with visual works of art. Both lectio divina and visio divina can be practiced individually or in group settings.

The Alabaster Guided Meditations combine lectio divina with visio divina, inviting us to contemplate the words of Scripture by way of the photographs that accompany the text. Readers can focus on the words of Scripture alone or add in the visual element, using the fourfold lectio divina pattern.

These meditations invite us to enter into Holy Scripture in a new way—not as a passive text to be studied, but as the living Word of God, spoken anew to us.

CREDITS

Author of Guided Meditations
Jan Johnson

Creative Director
Bryan Ye-Chung

Business Director
Brian Chung

Operations Director
Willa Jin

Product Designer
Tyler Zak

Special Thanks
Josephine Law

Photographers
Jacob Chung
Ian Teraoka
Bryan Ye-Chung

Models
GianCarlo Aguilar
Aaron Ashby
Calvin Boyd
Nick Kwok
Joshua Kwok
Mark Mekailian
Chris Miller
Clay Song
Jessica Ticas

1

PROLOGUE: CHRIST, THE ETERNAL WORD

[1] In the beginning the Word already existed. The Word was with God, and the Word was God. [2] He existed in the beginning with God. [3] God created everything through him, and nothing was created except through him. [4] The Word gave life to everything that was created, and his life brought light to everyone. [5] The light shines in the darkness, and the darkness can never extinguish it. [6] God sent a man, John the Baptist, [7] to tell about the light so that everyone might believe because of his testimony. [8] John himself was not the light; he was simply a witness to tell about the light. [9] The one who is the true light, who gives light to everyone, was coming into the world. [10] He came into the very world he created, but the world didn't recognize him. [11] He came to his own people, and even they rejected him. [12] But to all who believed him and accepted him, he gave the right to become children of God. [13] They are reborn—not with a physical birth resulting from human passion or plan, but a birth that comes from God. [14] So the Word became human and made his home among us. He was full of unfailing love and faithfulness. And we have seen his glory, the glory of the Father's one and only Son. [15] John testified about him when he shouted to the crowds, "This is the one I was talking about when I said, 'Someone is coming after me who is far greater than I am, for he existed long before me.'" [16] From his abundance we have all received one gracious blessing after another. [17] For the law was given through Moses, but God's unfailing love and faithfulness came through Jesus Christ. [18] No one has ever seen God. But the unique One, who is himself God, is near to the Father's heart. He has revealed God to us.

THE TESTIMONY OF JOHN THE BAPTIST

[19] This was John's testimony when the Jewish leaders sent priests and Temple assistants from Jerusalem to ask John, "Who are you?" [20] He came right out and said, "I am not the Messiah." [21] "Well then, who are you?" they asked. "Are you Elijah?" "No," he replied. "Are you the Prophet we are expecting?" "No." [22] "Then who are you? We need an answer for those who sent us. What do you have to say about yourself?" [23] John replied in the words of the prophet Isaiah: "I am a voice shouting in the wilderness, 'Clear the way for the LORD's coming!'" [24] Then the Pharisees who had been sent [25] asked him, "If you aren't the Messiah or Elijah or the Prophet, what right do you have to baptize?" [26] John told them, "I baptize with water, but right here in the crowd is someone you do not recognize. [27] Though his ministry follows mine, I'm not even worthy to be his slave and untie the straps of his sandal." [28] This encounter took place in Bethany, an area east of the Jordan River, where John was baptizing.

JESUS, THE LAMB OF GOD

[29] The next day John saw Jesus coming toward him and said, "Look! The Lamb of God who takes away the sin of the world! [30] He is the one I was talking about when I said, 'A man is coming after me who is far greater than I am, for he existed long before me.' [31] I did not recognize him as the Messiah, but I have been baptizing with water so that he might be revealed to Israel." [32] Then John testified, "I saw the Holy Spirit descending like a dove from heaven and resting upon him. [33] I didn't know he was the one, but when God sent me to baptize with water, he told me, 'The one on whom you see the Spirit descend and rest is the one who will baptize with the Holy Spirit.' [34] I saw this happen to Jesus, so I testify that he is the Chosen One of God."

THE FIRST DISCIPLES

[35] The following day John was again standing with two of his disciples. [36] As Jesus walked by, John looked at him and declared, "Look! There is the Lamb of God!" [37] When John's two disciples heard this, they followed Jesus. [38] Jesus looked around and saw them following. "What do you want?" he asked them. They replied, "Rabbi" (which means "Teacher"), "where are you staying?" [39] "Come and see," he said. It was about four o'clock in the afternoon when they went with him to the place where he was staying, and they remained with him the rest of the day. [40] Andrew, Simon Peter's brother, was one of these men who heard what John said and then followed Jesus. [41] Andrew went to find his brother, Simon, and told him, "We have found the Messiah" (which means "Christ"). [42] Then Andrew brought Simon to meet Jesus. Looking intently at Simon, Jesus said, "Your name is Simon, son of John—but you will be called Cephas" (which means "Peter"). [43] The next day Jesus decided to go to Galilee. He found Philip and said to him, "Come, follow me." [44] Philip was from Bethsaida, Andrew and Peter's hometown. [45] Philip went to look for Nathanael and told him, "We have found the very person Moses and the prophets wrote about! His name is Jesus, the son of Joseph from Nazareth." [46] "Nazareth!" exclaimed Nathanael. "Can anything good come from Nazareth?" "Come and see for yourself," Philip replied. [47] As they approached, Jesus said, "Now here is a genuine son of Israel—a man of complete integrity." [48] "How do you know about me?" Nathanael asked. Jesus replied, "I could see you under the fig tree before Philip found you." [49] Then Nathanael exclaimed, "Rabbi, you are the Son of God—the King of Israel!" [50] Jesus asked him, "Do you believe this just because I told you I had seen you under the fig tree? You will see greater things than this." [51] Then he said, "I tell you the truth, you will all see heaven open and the angels of God going up and down on the Son of Man, the one who is the stairway between heaven and earth."

2

THE WEDDING AT CANA

[1] The next day there was a wedding celebration in the village of Cana in Galilee. Jesus' mother was there, [2] and Jesus and his disciples were also invited to the celebration. [3] The wine supply ran out during the festivities, so Jesus' mother told him, "They have no more wine." [4] "Dear woman, that's not our problem," Jesus replied. "My time has not yet come." [5] But his mother told the servants, "Do whatever he tells you." [6] Standing nearby were six stone water jars, used for Jewish ceremonial washing. Each could hold twenty to thirty gallons. [7] Jesus told the servants, "Fill the jars with water." When the jars had been filled, [8] he said, "Now dip some out, and take it to the master of ceremonies." So the servants followed his instructions. [9] When the master of ceremonies tasted the water that was now wine, not knowing where it had come from (though, of course, the servants knew), he called the bridegroom over. [10] "A host always serves the best wine first," he said. "Then, when everyone has had a lot to drink, he brings out the less expensive wine. But you have kept the best until now!" [11] This miraculous sign at Cana in Galilee was the first time Jesus revealed his glory. And his disciples believed in him. [12] After the wedding he went to Capernaum for a few days with his mother, his brothers, and his disciples.

JESUS CLEARS THE TEMPLE

[13] It was nearly time for the Jewish Passover celebration, so Jesus went to Jerusalem. [14] In the Temple area he saw merchants selling cattle, sheep, and doves for sacrifices; he also saw dealers at tables exchanging foreign money. [15] Jesus made a whip from some ropes and chased them all out of the Temple. He drove out the sheep and cattle, scattered the money changers' coins over the floor, and turned over their tables. [16] Then, going over to the people who sold doves, he told them, "Get these things out of here. Stop turning my Father's house into a marketplace!" [17] Then his disciples remembered this prophecy from the Scriptures: "Passion for God's house will consume me." [18] But the Jewish leaders demanded, "What are you doing? If God gave you authority to do this, show us a miraculous sign to prove it." [19] "All right," Jesus replied. "Destroy this temple, and in three days I will raise it up." [20] "What!" they exclaimed. "It has taken forty-six years to build this Temple, and you can rebuild it in three days?" [21] But when Jesus said "this temple," he meant his own body. [22] After he was raised from the dead, his disciples remembered he had said this, and they believed both the Scriptures and what Jesus had said.

JESUS AND NICODEMUS

[23] Because of the miraculous signs Jesus did in Jerusalem at the Passover celebration, many began to trust in him. [24] But Jesus didn't trust them, because he knew all about people. [25] No one needed to tell him about human nature, for he knew what was in each person's heart.

THE WEDDING AT CANA

JOHN 2:1-12

READ

1. Read John 2:1-12 slowly (aloud, if it's not intrusive to others).
2. Look at the photo on page 6.
3. Pause.

REFLECT

1. Read the passage again, slowly.
2. Notice the details of the photo:
   - the dark Middle-Eastern hand almost caressing the wine glass
   - the thin stream of wine being poured
   - the water in the glass slowly being transformed to wine
   - the reflection of the red wine (or is that blood?) on the finger
3. What does this image suggest to you?
4. Read the passage again and notice what words or phrases resonate with you.

5. Ask God why that might be.
6. What, if anything, do you sense God inviting you to consider?

RESPOND

1. Position your hand as in the photo as if holding an elegant glass.
2. Say (aloud, if possible) your response to God about what stood out to you.
3. Perhaps you wish to be filled also with the rich life of God.

REST

1. Exhale.
2. Soak in the sense of what it might be like to be filled with all the fullness of God.
3. If you wish, cup your hands in front of you as an invitation to be filled with God.

3

[1] There was a man named Nicodemus, a Jewish religious leader who was a Pharisee. [2] After dark one evening, he came to speak with Jesus. "Rabbi," he said, "we all know that God has sent you to teach us. Your miraculous signs are evidence that God is with you." [3] Jesus replied, "I tell you the truth, unless you are born again, you cannot see the Kingdom of God." [4] "What do you mean?" exclaimed Nicodemus. "How can an old man go back into his mother's womb and be born again?" [5] Jesus replied, "I assure you, no one can enter the Kingdom of God without being born of water and the Spirit. [6] Humans can reproduce only human life, but the Holy Spirit gives birth to spiritual life. [7] So don't be surprised when I say, 'You must be born again.' [8] The wind blows wherever it wants. Just as you can hear the wind but can't tell where it comes from or where it is going, so you can't explain how people are born of the Spirit." [9] "How are these things possible?" Nicodemus asked. [10] Jesus replied, "You are a respected Jewish teacher, and yet you don't understand these things? [11] I assure you, we tell you what we know and have seen, and yet you won't believe our testimony. [12] But if you don't believe me when I tell you about earthly things, how can you possibly believe if I tell you about heavenly things? [13] No one has ever gone to heaven and returned. But the Son of Man has come down from heaven. [14] And as Moses lifted up the bronze snake on a pole in the wilderness, so the Son of Man must be lifted up, [15] so that everyone who believes in him will have eternal life. [16] For this is how God loved the world: He gave his one and only Son, so that everyone who believes in him will not perish but have eternal life. [17] God sent his Son into the world not to judge the world, but to save the world through him. [18] There is no judgment against anyone who believes in him. But anyone who does not believe in him has already been judged for not believing in God's one and only Son. [19] And the judgment is based on this fact: God's light came into the world, but people loved the darkness more than the light, for their actions were evil. [20] All who do evil hate the light and refuse to go near it for fear their sins will be exposed. [21] But those who do what is right come to the light so others can see that they are doing what God wants."

THE WIND OF THE SPIRIT

JOHN 3:5-8

READ

1. Read John 3:1-8 slowly (aloud, if it's not intrusive to others). Pause and read aloud verses 5-8.
2. Look at the photos on page 10.
3. Pause.

REFLECT

1. Read again verses 5-8, slowly.
2. Pause.
3. Notice the contrasts between the two photos: colors, cloud formations, feelings they evoke.
4. How might one or both of these photos match the feelings Nicodemus may have had in hearing Jesus' words in verses 5-8?
5. How do one or both photos match your image of how the Holy Spirit works in your life?
6. Read the passage again and notice what words or phrases resonate with you.
7. Ask God why that might be.
8. What, if anything, do you sense God inviting you to consider, especially about how the Holy Spirit is working in your life? To feel? To do?

RESPOND

1. Tell God your responses to what stood out to you in the passage.
2. Note especially your response to the Spirit and the Spirit's activity in birthing new life.
3. If you have experienced any small rebirthing by the Spirit recently, describe that.
4. Describe also any rebirthing from the Spirit you would like to experience.
5. Tell God that too.
6. If you wish, include any requests regarding the Spirit's work within and around you.

REST

1. Read aloud John 3:5-8 one last time.
2. Rest in the knowledge that the Spirit of God dwells in people (Romans 8:9).
3. Dream for a moment what it would be like to live in a state of life in which you are transformed by the Spirit.

JOHN THE BAPTIST EXALTS JESUS

[22] Then Jesus and his disciples left Jerusalem and went into the Judean countryside. Jesus spent some time with them there, baptizing people. [23] At this time John the Baptist was baptizing at Aenon, near Salim, because there was plenty of water there; and people kept coming to him for baptism. [24] (This was before John was thrown into prison.) [25] A debate broke out between John's disciples and a certain Jew over ceremonial cleansing. [26] So John's disciples came to him and said, "Rabbi, the man you met on the other side of the Jordan River, the one you identified as the Messiah, is also baptizing people. And everybody is going to him instead of coming to us." [27] John replied, "No one can receive anything unless God gives it from heaven. [28] You yourselves know how plainly I told you, 'I am not the Messiah. I am only here to prepare the way for him.' [29] It is the bridegroom who marries the bride, and the bridegroom's friend is simply glad to stand with him and hear his vows. Therefore, I am filled with joy at his success. [30] He must become greater and greater, and I must become less and less. [31] He has come from above and is greater than anyone else. We are of the earth, and we speak of earthly things, but he has come from heaven and is greater than anyone else. [32] He testifies about what he has seen and heard, but how few believe what he tells them! [33] Anyone who accepts his testimony can affirm that God is true. [34] For he is sent by God. He speaks God's words, for God gives him the Spirit without limit. [35] The Father loves his Son and has put everything into his hands. [36] And anyone who believes in God's Son has eternal life. Anyone who doesn't obey the Son will never experience eternal life but remains under God's angry judgment."

4

JESUS AND THE SAMARITAN WOMAN

[1] Jesus knew the Pharisees had heard that he was baptizing and making more disciples than John [2] (though Jesus himself didn't baptize them—his disciples did). [3] So he left Judea and returned to Galilee. [4] He had to go through Samaria on the way. [5] Eventually he came to the Samaritan village of Sychar, near the field that Jacob gave to his son Joseph. [6] Jacob's well was there; and Jesus, tired from the long walk, sat wearily beside the well about noontime. [7] Soon a Samaritan woman came to draw water, and Jesus said to her, "Please give me a drink." [8] He was alone at the time because his disciples had gone into the village to buy some food. [9] The woman was surprised, for Jews refuse to have anything to do with Samaritans. She said to Jesus, "You are a Jew, and I am a Samaritan woman. Why are you asking me for a drink?" [10] Jesus replied, "If you only knew the gift God has for you and who you are speaking to, you would ask me, and I would give you living water." [11] "But sir, you don't have a rope or a bucket," she said, "and this well is very deep. Where would you get this living water? [12] And besides, do you think you're greater than our ancestor Jacob, who gave us this well? How can you offer better water than he and his sons and his animals enjoyed?" [13] Jesus replied, "Anyone who drinks this water will soon become thirsty again. [14] But those who drink the water I give will never be thirsty again. It becomes a fresh, bubbling spring within them, giving them eternal

life." ¹⁵ "Please, sir," the woman said, "give me this water! Then I'll never be thirsty again, and I won't have to come here to get water." ¹⁶ "Go and get your husband," Jesus told her. ¹⁷ "I don't have a husband," the woman replied. Jesus said, "You're right! You don't have a husband— ¹⁸ for you have had five husbands, and you aren't even married to the man you're living with now. You certainly spoke the truth!" ¹⁹ "Sir," the woman said, "you must be a prophet. ²⁰ So tell me, why is it that you Jews insist that Jerusalem is the only place of worship, while we Samaritans claim it is here at Mount Gerizim, where our ancestors worshiped?" ²¹ Jesus replied, "Believe me, dear woman, the time is coming when it will no longer matter whether you worship the Father on this mountain or in Jerusalem. ²² You Samaritans know very little about the one you worship, while we Jews know all about him, for salvation comes through the Jews. ²³ But the time is coming—indeed it's here now—when true worshipers will worship the Father in spirit and in truth. The Father is looking for those who will worship him that way. ²⁴ For God is Spirit, so those who worship him must worship in spirit and in truth." ²⁵ The woman said, "I know the Messiah is coming—the one who is called Christ. When he comes, he will explain everything to us." ²⁶ Then Jesus told her, "I am the Messiah!" [27] Just then his disciples came back. They were shocked to find him talking to a woman, but none of them had the nerve to ask, "What do you want with her?" or "Why are you talking to her?" [28] The woman left her water jar beside the well and ran back to the village, telling everyone, [29] "Come and see a man who told me everything I ever did! Could he possibly be the Messiah?" [30] So the people came streaming from the village to see him. [31] Meanwhile, the disciples were urging Jesus, "Rabbi, eat something." [32] But Jesus replied, "I have a kind of food you know nothing about." [33] "Did someone bring him food while we were gone?" the disciples asked each other. [34] Then Jesus explained: "My nourishment comes from doing the will of God, who sent me, and from finishing his work. [35] You know the saying, 'Four months between planting and harvest.' But I say, wake up and look around. The fields are already ripe for harvest. [36] The harvesters are paid good wages, and the fruit they harvest is people brought to eternal life. What joy awaits both the planter and the harvester alike! [37] You know the saying, 'One plants and another harvests.' And it's true. [38] I sent you to harvest where you didn't plant; others had already done the work, and now you will get to gather the harvest."

MANY SAMARITANS BELIEVE

[39] Many Samaritans from the village believed in Jesus because the woman had said, "He told me everything I ever did!" [40] When they came out to see him, they begged him to stay in their village. So he stayed for two days, [41] long enough for many more to hear his message and believe. [42] Then they said to the woman, "Now we believe, not just because of what you told us, but because we have heard him ourselves. Now we know that he is indeed the Savior of the world."

JESUS HEALS AN OFFICIAL'S SON

[43] At the end of the two days, Jesus went on to Galilee. [44] He himself had said that a prophet is not honored in his own hometown. [45] Yet the Galileans welcomed him, for they had been in Jerusalem at the Passover celebration and had seen everything he did there. [46] As he traveled through Galilee, he came to Cana, where he had turned the water into wine. There was a government official in nearby Capernaum whose son was very sick. [47] When he heard that Jesus had come from Judea to Galilee, he went and begged Jesus to come to Capernaum to heal his son, who was about to die. [48] Jesus asked, "Will you never believe in me unless you see miraculous signs and wonders?" [49] The official pleaded, "Lord, please come now before my little boy dies." [50] Then Jesus told him, "Go back home. Your son will live!" And the man believed what Jesus said and started home. [51] While the man was on his way, some of his servants met him with the news that his son was alive and well. [52] He asked them when the boy had begun to get better, and they replied, "Yesterday afternoon at one o'clock his fever suddenly disappeared!" [53] Then the father realized that that was the very time Jesus had told him, "Your son will live." And he and his entire household believed in Jesus. [54] This was the second miraculous sign Jesus did in Galilee after coming from Judea.

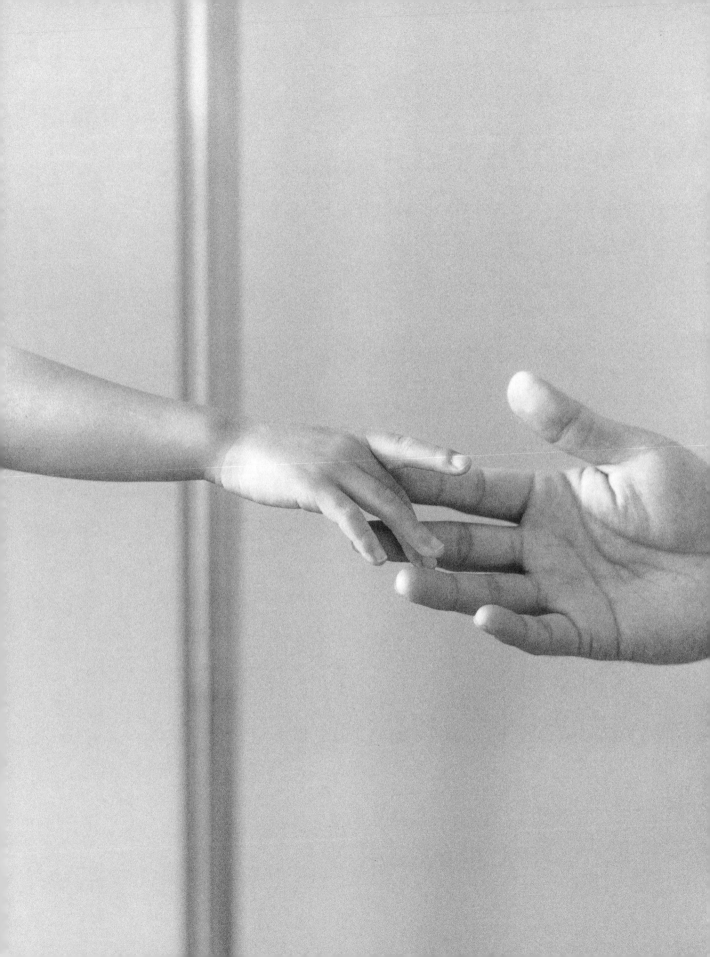

JESUS HEALS AN OFFICIAL'S SON

JOHN 4:46-54

READ

1. Read John 4:46-54 slowly (aloud, if it's not intrusive to others).
2. Look at the photo on page 19.
3. Pause.

REFLECT

1. Read the text again, slowly.
2. Notice the details of the photo, especially how the hands differ.
3. One is young; the other is older.
4. The one on the left is pale and obviously pampered; the one on the right is darker.
5. Notice the black on the underside of the fingers and hand. Might this be the color of the power rushing through the hand?
6. How does this photo accentuate the differences between Jesus and the government official and his son?
7. What barriers (notice the white and yellow vertical lines) did Jesus' love cross in this healing?
8. Pause.
9. Read the passage again and notice what stands out to you.

10. What words or phrases resonate with you?
11. Notice if you perhaps find that you identify with the hand on the left or right.
12. If so, is someone reaching out for you, or are you reaching out for someone?
13. Ask God why that might be.
14. What, if anything, do you sense God inviting you to consider? To feel? To do?

RESPOND

1. Reach out your hand as if moving beyond some barrier.
2. Say (aloud, if possible) your response to God about what stood out to you.
3. If you sensed yourself in one of the hands, describe what you're reaching for.
4. If you need God's help in this, say that as well.

REST

1. Read aloud the verse or word or phrase that stood out to you.
2. Exhale.
3. Soak in the idea of connecting with God and others across distances and barriers.

5

JESUS HEALS A LAME MAN

¹ Afterward Jesus returned to Jerusalem for one of the Jewish holy days.
² Inside the city, near the Sheep Gate, was the pool of Bethesda, with
five covered porches. ³ Crowds of sick people—blind, lame, or paralyzed—
lay on the porches. ⁵ One of the men lying there had been sick for
thirty-eight years. ⁶ When Jesus saw him and knew he had been ill for a
long time, he asked him, "Would you like to get well?" ⁷ "I can't, sir,"
the sick man said, "for I have no one to put me into the pool when the
water bubbles up. Someone else always gets there ahead of me." ⁸ Jesus
told him, "Stand up, pick up your mat, and walk!" ⁹ Instantly, the man
was healed! He rolled up his sleeping mat and began walking! But this
miracle happened on the Sabbath, ¹⁰ so the Jewish leaders objected.
They said to the man who was cured, "You can't work on the Sabbath!
The law doesn't allow you to carry that sleeping mat!" ¹¹ But he replied,
"The man who healed me told me, 'Pick up your mat and walk.'"
¹² "Who said such a thing as that?" they demanded. ¹³ The man didn't
know, for Jesus had disappeared into the crowd. ¹⁴ But afterward Jesus
found him in the Temple and told him, "Now you are well; so stop
sinning, or something even worse may happen to you." ¹⁵ Then the man
went and told the Jewish leaders that it was Jesus who had healed him.

JESUS HEALS A LAME MAN

JOHN 5:1-15

READ

1. Read John 5:1-15 slowly (aloud, if it's not intrusive to others).
2. Look at the photo on page 23.

REFLECT

1. Read again, slowly.
2. Pause.
3. Look again at the photo.
4. What do you notice?
5. In the photo, observe how the hand grasps the mat firmly.
6. What might the healed man have been feeling as he grasped the mat (v. 9)?
7. Read the passage again and notice what stands out to you.
8. What words or phrases resonate with you?

9. Ask God why that might be.
10. What, if anything, do you sense God inviting you to consider? To feel? To do?

RESPOND

1. Stand up and imagine for a moment that you have not stood up straight for thirty-eight years.
2. What might this be like?
3. If this were your situation, what would you want to say to God?
4. Tell God what, if anything, you're being invited to grasp, to take hold of, to adventure forth about.

REST

1. Exhale.
2. Soak in the idea of God being equipped to move forward, even if others object.

JESUS CLAIMS TO BE THE SON OF GOD

¹⁶ So the Jewish leaders began harassing Jesus for breaking the Sabbath rules. ¹⁷ But Jesus replied, "My Father is always working, and so am I." ¹⁸ So the Jewish leaders tried all the harder to find a way to kill him. For he not only broke the Sabbath, he called God his Father, thereby making himself equal with God. ¹⁹ So Jesus explained, "I tell you the truth, the Son can do nothing by himself. He does only what he sees the Father doing. Whatever the Father does, the Son also does. ²⁰ For the Father loves the Son and shows him everything he is doing. In fact, the Father will show him how to do even greater works than healing this man. Then you will truly be astonished. ²¹ For just as the Father gives life to those he raises from the dead, so the Son gives life to anyone he wants. ²² In addition, the Father judges no one. Instead, he has given the Son absolute authority to judge, ²³ so that everyone will honor the Son, just as they honor the Father. Anyone who does not honor the Son is certainly not honoring the Father who sent him. ²⁴ I tell you the truth, those who listen to my message and believe in God who sent me have eternal life. They will never be condemned for their sins, but they have already passed from death into life. ²⁵ And I assure you that the time is coming, indeed it's here now, when the dead will hear my voice—the voice of the Son of God. And those who listen will live. ²⁶ The Father has life in himself, and he has granted that same life-giving power to his Son. ²⁷ And he has given him authority to judge everyone because he is the Son of Man. ²⁸ Don't be so surprised! Indeed, the time is coming when all the dead in their graves will hear the voice of God's Son, ²⁹ and they will rise again. Those who have done good will rise to experience eternal life, and those who have continued in evil will rise to experience judgment. ³⁰ I can do nothing on my own. I judge as God tells me. Therefore, my judgment is just, because I carry out the will of the one who sent me, not my own will.

WITNESSES TO JESUS

³¹ "If I were to testify on my own behalf, my testimony would not be valid. ³² But someone else is also testifying about me, and I assure you that everything he says about me is true. ³³ In fact, you sent investigators to listen to John the Baptist, and his testimony about me was true. ³⁴ Of course, I have no need of human witnesses, but I say these things so you might be saved. ³⁵ John was like a burning and shining lamp, and you were excited for a while about his message. ³⁶ But I have a greater witness than John—my teachings and my miracles. The Father gave me these works to accomplish, and they prove that he sent me. ³⁷ And the Father who sent me has testified about me himself. You have never heard his voice or seen him face to face, ³⁸ and you do not have his message in your hearts, because you do not believe me—the one he sent to you. ³⁹ You search the Scriptures because you think they give you eternal life. But the Scriptures point to me! ⁴⁰ Yet you refuse to come to me to receive this life. ⁴¹ Your approval means nothing to me, ⁴² because I know you don't have God's love within you. ⁴³ For I have come to you in my Father's name, and you have rejected me. Yet if others come in their own name, you gladly welcome them. ⁴⁴ No wonder you can't believe! For you gladly honor each other, but you don't care about the honor that comes from the one who alone is God. ⁴⁵ Yet it isn't I who will accuse you before the Father. Moses will accuse you! Yes, Moses, in whom you put your hopes. ⁴⁶ If you really believed Moses, you would believe me, because he wrote about me. ⁴⁷ But since you don't believe what he wrote, how will you believe what I say?"

6

JESUS FEEDS FIVE THOUSAND

[1] After this, Jesus crossed over to the far side of the Sea of Galilee, also known as the Sea of Tiberias. [2] A huge crowd kept following him wherever he went, because they saw his miraculous signs as he healed the sick. [3] Then Jesus climbed a hill and sat down with his disciples around him. [4] (It was nearly time for the Jewish Passover celebration.) [5] Jesus soon saw a huge crowd of people coming to look for him. Turning to Philip, he asked, "Where can we buy bread to feed all these people?" [6] He was testing Philip, for he already knew what he was going to do. [7] Philip replied, "Even if we worked for months, we wouldn't have enough money to feed them!" [8] Then Andrew, Simon Peter's brother, spoke up. [9] "There's a young boy here with five barley loaves and two fish. But what good is that with this huge crowd?" [10] "Tell everyone to sit down," Jesus said. So they all sat down on the grassy slopes. (The men alone numbered about 5,000.) [11] Then Jesus took the loaves, gave thanks to God, and distributed them to the people. Afterward he did the same with the fish. And they all ate as much as they wanted. [12] After everyone was full, Jesus told his disciples, "Now gather the leftovers, so that nothing is wasted." [13] So they picked up the pieces and filled twelve baskets with scraps left by the people who had eaten from the five barley loaves. [14] When the people saw him do this miraculous sign, they exclaimed, "Surely, he is the Prophet we have been expecting!" [15] When Jesus saw that they were ready to force him to be their king, he slipped away into the hills by himself.

JESUS WALKS ON WATER

[16] That evening Jesus' disciples went down to the shore to wait for him. [17] But as darkness fell and Jesus still hadn't come back, they got into the boat and headed across the lake toward Capernaum. [18] Soon a gale swept down upon them, and the sea grew very rough. [19] They had rowed three or four miles when suddenly they saw Jesus walking on the water toward the boat. They were terrified, [20] but he called out to them, "Don't be afraid. I am here!" [21] Then they were eager to let him in the boat, and immediately they arrived at their destination!

JESUS, THE BREAD OF LIFE

22 The next day the crowd that had stayed on the far shore saw that the disciples had taken the only boat, and they realized Jesus had not gone with them. 23 Several boats from Tiberias landed near the place where the Lord had blessed the bread and the people had eaten. 24 So when the crowd saw that neither Jesus nor his disciples were there, they got into the boats and went across to Capernaum to look for him. 25 They found him on the other side of the lake and asked, "Rabbi, when did you get here?" 26 Jesus replied, "I tell you the truth, you want to be with me because I fed you, not because you understood the miraculous signs. 27 But don't be so concerned about perishable things like food. Spend your energy seeking the eternal life that the Son of Man can give you. For God the Father has given me the seal of his approval." 28 They replied, "We want to perform God's works, too. What should we do?" 29 Jesus told them, "This is the only work God wants from you: Believe in the one he has sent." 30 They answered, "Show us a miraculous sign if you want us to believe in you. What can you do? 31 After all, our ancestors ate manna while they journeyed through the wilderness! The Scriptures say, 'Moses gave them bread from heaven to eat.'" 32 Jesus said, "I tell you the truth, Moses didn't give you bread from heaven. My Father did. And now he offers you the true bread from heaven. 33 The true bread of God is the one who comes down from heaven and gives life to the world." 34 "Sir," they said, "give us that bread every day." 35 Jesus replied, "I am the bread of life. Whoever comes to me will never be hungry again. Whoever believes in me will never be thirsty. 36 But you haven't believed in me even though you have seen me. 37 However, those the Father has given me will come to me, and I will never reject them. 38 For I have come down from heaven to do the will of God who sent me, not to do my own will. 39 And this is the will of God, that I should not lose even one of all those he has given me, but that I should raise them up at the last day. 40 For it is my Father's will that all who see his Son and believe in him should have eternal life. I will raise them up at the last day." 41 Then the people began to murmur in disagreement because he had said, "I am the bread that came down from heaven." 42 They said, "Isn't this Jesus, the son of Joseph? We know his father and mother. How can he say, 'I came down from heaven'?" 43 But Jesus replied, "Stop complaining about what I said. 44 For no one can come to me unless the Father who sent me draws them to me, and at the last day I will raise them up. 45 As it is written in the Scriptures, 'They will all be taught by God.' Everyone who listens to the Father and learns from him comes to me. 46 (Not that anyone has ever seen the Father; only I, who was sent from God, have seen him.) 47 I tell you the truth, anyone who believes has eternal life. 48 Yes, I am the bread of life! 49 Your ancestors ate manna in the wilderness, but they all died. 50 Anyone who eats the bread from heaven, however, will never die. 51 I am the living bread that came down from heaven. Anyone who eats this bread will live forever; and this bread, which I will offer so the world may live, is my flesh." 52 Then the people began arguing with each other about what he meant. "How can this man give us his flesh to eat?" they asked. 53 So Jesus said again, "I tell you the truth, unless you eat the flesh of the Son of Man and drink his blood, you cannot have eternal life within you. 54 But anyone who eats my flesh and drinks my blood has eternal life, and I will raise that person at the last day. 55 For my flesh is true food, and my blood is true drink. 56 Anyone who eats my flesh and drinks my blood remains in me, and I in him. 57 I live because of the living Father who sent me; in the same way, anyone who feeds on me will live because of me. 58 I am the true bread that came down from heaven. Anyone who eats this bread will not die as your ancestors did (even though they ate the manna) but will live forever." 59 He said these things while he was teaching in the synagogue in Capernaum.

MANY DISCIPLES DESERT JESUS

[60] Many of his disciples said, "This is very hard to understand. How can anyone accept it?" [61] Jesus was aware that his disciples were complaining, so he said to them, "Does this offend you? [62] Then what will you think if you see the Son of Man ascend to heaven again? [63] The Spirit alone gives eternal life. Human effort accomplishes nothing. And the very words I have spoken to you are spirit and life. [64] But some of you do not believe me." (For Jesus knew from the beginning which ones didn't believe, and he knew who would betray him.) [65] Then he said, "That is why I said that people can't come to me unless the Father gives them to me." [66] At this point many of his disciples turned away and deserted him. [67] Then Jesus turned to the Twelve and asked, "Are you also going to leave?" [68] Simon Peter replied, "Lord, to whom would we go? You have the words that give eternal life. [69] We believe, and we know you are the Holy One of God." [70] Then Jesus said, "I chose the twelve of you, but one is a devil." [71] He was speaking of Judas, son of Simon Iscariot, one of the Twelve, who would later betray him.

7

JESUS AND HIS BROTHERS

[1] After this, Jesus traveled around Galilee. He wanted to stay out of Judea, where the Jewish leaders were plotting his death. [2] But soon it was time for the Jewish Festival of Shelters, [3] and Jesus' brothers said to him, "Leave here and go to Judea, where your followers can see your miracles! [4] You can't become famous if you hide like this! If you can do such wonderful things, show yourself to the world!" [5] For even his brothers didn't believe in him. [6] Jesus replied, "Now is not the right time for me to go, but you can go anytime. [7] The world can't hate you, but it does hate me because I accuse it of doing evil. [8] You go on. I'm not going to this festival, because my time has not yet come." [9] After saying these things, Jesus remained in Galilee.

JESUS TEACHES OPENLY AT THE TEMPLE

[10] But after his brothers left for the festival, Jesus also went, though secretly, staying out of public view. [11] The Jewish leaders tried to find him at the festival and kept asking if anyone had seen him. [12] There was a lot of grumbling about him among the crowds. Some argued, "He's a good man," but others said, "He's nothing but a fraud who deceives the people." [13] But no one had the courage to speak favorably about him in public, for they were afraid of getting in trouble with the Jewish leaders. [14] Then, midway through the festival, Jesus went up to the Temple and began to teach. [15] The people were surprised when they heard him. "How does he know so much when he hasn't been trained?" they asked. [16] So Jesus told them, "My message is not my own; it comes from God who sent me. [17] Anyone who wants to do the will of God will know whether my teaching is from God or is merely my own. [18] Those who speak for themselves want glory only for themselves, but a person who seeks to honor the one who sent him speaks truth, not lies. [19] Moses gave you the law, but none of you obeys it! In fact, you are trying to kill me." [20] The crowd replied, "You're demon possessed! Who's trying to kill you?" [21] Jesus replied, "I did one miracle on the Sabbath, and you were amazed. [22] But you work on the Sabbath, too, when you obey Moses' law of circumcision. (Actually, this tradition of circumcision began with the patriarchs, long before the law of Moses.) [23] For if the correct time for circumcising your son falls on the Sabbath, you go ahead and do it so as not to break the law of Moses. So why should you be angry with me for healing a man on the Sabbath? [24] Look beneath the surface so you can judge correctly."

IS JESUS THE MESSIAH?

²⁵ Some of the people who lived in Jerusalem started to ask each other, "Isn't this the man they are trying to kill? ²⁶ But here he is, speaking in public, and they say nothing to him. Could our leaders possibly believe that he is the Messiah? ²⁷ But how could he be? For we know where this man comes from. When the Messiah comes, he will simply appear; no one will know where he comes from." ²⁸ While Jesus was teaching in the Temple, he called out, "Yes, you know me, and you know where I come from. But I'm not here on my own. The one who sent me is true, and you don't know him. ²⁹ But I know him because I come from him, and he sent me to you." ³⁰ Then the leaders tried to arrest him; but no one laid a hand on him, because his time had not yet come. ³¹ Many among the crowds at the Temple believed in him. "After all," they said, "would you expect the Messiah to do more miraculous signs than this man has done?" ³² When the Pharisees heard that the crowds were whispering such things, they and the leading priests sent Temple guards to arrest Jesus. ³³ But Jesus told them, "I will be with you only a little longer. Then I will return to the one who sent me. ³⁴ You will search for me but not find me. And you cannot go where I am going." ³⁵ The Jewish leaders were puzzled by this statement. "Where is he planning to go?" they asked. "Is he thinking of leaving the country and going to the Jews in other lands? Maybe he will even teach the Greeks! ³⁶ What does he mean when he says, 'You will search for me but not find me,' and 'You cannot go where I am going'?"

JESUS PROMISES LIVING WATER

³⁷ On the last day, the climax of the festival, Jesus stood and shouted to the crowds, "Anyone who is thirsty may come to me! ³⁸ Anyone who believes in me may come and drink! For the Scriptures declare, 'Rivers of living water will flow from his heart.'" ³⁹ (When he said "living water," he was speaking of the Spirit, who would be given to everyone believing in him. But the Spirit had not yet been given, because Jesus had not yet entered into his glory.)

DIVISION AND UNBELIEF

⁴⁰ When the crowds heard him say this, some of them declared, "Surely this man is the Prophet we've been expecting." ⁴¹ Others said, "He is the Messiah." Still others said, "But he can't be! Will the Messiah come from Galilee? ⁴² For the Scriptures clearly state that the Messiah will be born of the royal line of David, in Bethlehem, the village where King David was born." ⁴³ So the crowd was divided about him. ⁴⁴ Some even wanted him arrested, but no one laid a hand on him. ⁴⁵ When the Temple guards returned without having arrested Jesus, the leading priests and Pharisees demanded, "Why didn't you bring him in?" ⁴⁶ "We have never heard anyone speak like this!" the guards responded. ⁴⁷ "Have you been led astray, too?" the Pharisees mocked. ⁴⁸ "Is there a single one of us rulers or Pharisees who believes in him? ⁴⁹ This foolish crowd follows him, but they are ignorant of the law. God's curse is on them!" ⁵⁰ Then Nicodemus, the leader who had met with Jesus earlier, spoke up. ⁵¹ "Is it legal to convict a man before he is given a hearing?" he asked. ⁵² They replied, "Are you from Galilee, too? Search the Scriptures and see for yourself—no prophet ever comes from Galilee!"

8

A WOMAN CAUGHT IN ADULTERY

[1] Jesus returned to the Mount of Olives, [2] but early the next morning he was back again at the Temple. A crowd soon gathered, and he sat down and taught them. [3] As he was speaking, the teachers of religious law and the Pharisees brought a woman who had been caught in the act of adultery. They put her in front of the crowd. [4] "Teacher," they said to Jesus, "this woman was caught in the act of adultery. [5] The law of Moses says to stone her. What do you say?"[6] They were trying to trap him into saying something they could use against him, but Jesus stooped down and wrote in the dust with his finger. [7] They kept demanding an answer, so he stood up again and said, "All right, but let the one who has never sinned throw the first stone!" [8] Then he stooped down again and wrote in the dust. [9] When the accusers heard this, they slipped away one by one, beginning with the oldest, until only Jesus was left in the middle of the crowd with the woman. [10] Then Jesus stood up again and said to the woman, "Where are your accusers? Didn't even one of them condemn you?" [11] "No, Lord," she said. And Jesus said, "Neither do I. Go and sin no more."

A WOMAN CAUGHT IN ADULTERY

JOHN 8:1-11

READ

1. Read John 8:1-11 slowly (aloud, if it's not intrusive to others).
2. Look at the photo across the page on page 38.
3. Pause.

REFLECT

1. Read the text again, slowly.
2. In the photo, notice the position of the hand holding the rock in the air, almost as if it were a camera and she was taking a selfie.
3. What would you guess that the woman in the photo is feeling as she gazes at that rock?
4. Consider the rocks being held in the hands of people or situations around you and how they're poised to destroy something.
5. What might Jesus say about these?
6. Read the passage again and put yourself into this scene.
7. Notice what moment in the narrative stands out to you.
8. Do you perhaps identify with the woman or the people in the crowd, or are you simply a bystander?
9. What words or phrases resonate with you?
10. What feelings come to you?
11. What, if anything, do you sense God inviting you to consider? To do?

RESPOND

1. Tell God how it feels to have Christ intervene for someone who is not innocent, to be defended and then empowered to obey.
2. Ask God to help you in any situation that is similar to this.
3. Let this prayer pour forth from you—perhaps gently, perhaps passionately.

REST

1. Rest in the grace and joy of being pardoned and empowered to do what is right.
2. Exhale.

JESUS, THE LIGHT OF THE WORLD

[12] Jesus spoke to the people once more and said, "I am the light of the world. If you follow me, you won't have to walk in darkness, because you will have the light that leads to life." [13] The Pharisees replied, "You are making those claims about yourself! Such testimony is not valid." [14] Jesus told them, "These claims are valid even though I make them about myself. For I know where I came from and where I am going, but you don't know this about me. [15] You judge me by human standards, but I do not judge anyone. [16] And if I did, my judgment would be correct in every respect because I am not alone. The Father who sent me is with me. [17] Your own law says that if two people agree about something, their witness is accepted as fact. [18] I am one witness, and my Father who sent me is the other." [19] "Where is your father?" they asked. Jesus answered, "Since you don't know who I am, you don't know who my Father is. If you knew me, you would also know my Father." [20] Jesus made these statements while he was teaching in the section of the Temple known as the Treasury. But he was not arrested, because his time had not yet come.

THE UNBELIEVING PEOPLE WARNED

[21] Later Jesus said to them again, "I am going away. You will search for me but will die in your sin. You cannot come where I am going." [22] The people asked, "Is he planning to commit suicide? What does he mean, 'You cannot come where I am going'?" [23] Jesus continued, "You are from below; I am from above. You belong to this world; I do not. [24] That is why I said that you will die in your sins; for unless you believe that I am who I claim to be, you will die in your sins." [25] "Who are you?" they demanded. Jesus replied, "The one I have always claimed to be. [26] I have much to say about you and much to condemn, but I won't. For I say only what I have heard from the one who sent me, and he is completely truthful." [27] But they still didn't understand that he was talking about his Father. [28] So Jesus said, "When you have lifted up the Son of Man on the cross, then you will understand that I AM he. I do nothing on my own but say only what the Father taught me. [29] And the one who sent me is with me—he has not deserted me. For I always do what pleases him." [30] Then many who heard him say these things believed in him.

JESUS AND ABRAHAM

[31] Jesus said to the people who believed in him, "You are truly my disciples if you remain faithful to my teachings. [32] And you will know the truth, and the truth will set you free." [33] "But we are descendants of Abraham," they said. "We have never been slaves to anyone. What do you mean, 'You will be set free'?" [34] Jesus replied, "I tell you the truth, everyone who sins is a slave of sin. [35] A slave is not a permanent member of the family, but a son is part of the family forever. [36] So if the Son sets you free, you are truly free. [37] Yes, I realize that you are descendants of Abraham. And yet some of you are trying to kill me because there's no room in your hearts for my message. [38] I am telling you what I saw when I was with my Father. But you are following the advice of your father." [39] "Our father is Abraham!" they declared. "No," Jesus replied, "for if you were really the children of Abraham, you would follow his example. [40] Instead, you are trying to kill me because I told you the truth, which I heard from God. Abraham never did such a thing. [41] No, you are imitating your real father." They replied, "We aren't illegitimate children! God himself is our true Father." [42] Jesus told them, "If God were your Father, you would love me, because I have come to you from God. I am not here on my own, but he sent me. [43] Why can't you understand what I am saying? It's because you can't even hear me! [44] For you are the children of your father the devil, and you love to do the evil things he does. He was a murderer from the beginning. He has always hated the truth, because there is no truth in him. When he lies, it is consistent with his character; for he is a liar and the father of lies. [45] So when I tell the truth, you just naturally don't believe me! [46] Which of you can truthfully accuse me of sin? And since I am telling you the truth, why don't you believe me? [47] Anyone who belongs to God listens gladly to the words of God. But you don't listen because you don't belong to God." [48] The people retorted, "You Samaritan devil! Didn't we say all along that you were possessed by a demon?" [49] "No," Jesus said, "I have no demon in me. For I honor my Father—and you dishonor me. [50] And though I have no wish to glorify myself, God is going to glorify me. He is the true judge. [51] I tell you the truth, anyone who obeys my teaching will never die!" [52] The people said, "Now we know you are possessed by a demon. Even Abraham and the prophets died, but you say, 'Anyone who obeys my teaching will never die!' [53] Are you greater than our father Abraham? He died, and so did the prophets. Who do you think you are?" [54] Jesus answered, "If I want glory for myself, it doesn't count. But it is my Father who will glorify me. You say, 'He is our God,' [55] but you don't even know him. I know him. If I said otherwise, I would be as great a liar as you! But I do know him and obey him. [56] Your father Abraham rejoiced as he looked forward to my coming. He saw it and was glad." [57] The people said, "You aren't even fifty years old. How can you say you have seen Abraham?" [58] Jesus answered, "I tell you the truth, before Abraham was even born, I AM!" [59] At that point they picked up stones to throw at him. But Jesus was hidden from them and left the Temple.

9

JESUS HEALS A MAN BORN BLIND

¹ As Jesus was walking along, he saw a man who had been blind from birth. ² "Rabbi," his disciples asked him, "why was this man born blind? Was it because of his own sins or his parents' sins?" ³ "It was not because of his sins or his parents' sins," Jesus answered. "This happened so the power of God could be seen in him. ⁴ We must quickly carry out the tasks assigned us by the one who sent us. The night is coming, and then no one can work. ⁵ But while I am here in the world, I am the light of the world." ⁶ Then he spit on the ground, made mud with the saliva, and spread the mud over the blind man's eyes. ⁷ He told him, "Go wash yourself in the pool of Siloam" (Siloam means "sent"). So the man went and washed and came back seeing! ⁸ His neighbors and others who knew him as a blind beggar asked each other, "Isn't this the man who used to sit and beg?" ⁹ Some said he was, and others said, "No, he just looks like him!" But the beggar kept saying, "Yes, I am the same one!" ¹⁰ They asked, "Who healed you? What happened?" ¹¹ He told them, "The man they call Jesus made mud and spread it over my eyes and told me, 'Go to the pool of Siloam and wash yourself.' So I went and washed, and now I can see!" ¹² "Where is he now?" they asked. "I don't know," he replied. ¹³ Then they took the man who had been blind to the Pharisees, ¹⁴ because it was on the Sabbath that Jesus had made the mud and healed him. ¹⁵ The Pharisees asked the man all about it. So he told them, "He put the mud over my eyes, and when I washed it away, I could see!" ¹⁶ Some of the Pharisees said, "This man Jesus is not from God, for he is working on the Sabbath." Others said, "But how could an ordinary sinner do such miraculous signs?" So there was a deep division of opinion among them. ¹⁷ Then the Pharisees again questioned the man who had been blind and demanded, "What's your opinion about this man who healed you?" The man replied, "I think he must be a prophet." ¹⁸ The Jewish leaders still refused to believe the man had been blind and could now see, so they called in his parents. ¹⁹ They asked them, "Is this your son? Was he born blind? If so, how can he now see?" ²⁰ His parents replied, "We know this is our son and that he was born blind, ²¹ but we don't know how he can see or who healed him. Ask him. He is old enough to speak for himself." ²² His parents said this because they were afraid of the Jewish leaders, who had announced that anyone saying Jesus was the Messiah would be expelled from the synagogue. ²³ That's why they said, "He is old enough. Ask him." ²⁴ So for the second time they called in the man who had been blind and told him, "God should get the glory for this, because we know this man Jesus is a sinner." ²⁵ "I don't know whether he is a sinner," the man replied. "But I know this: I was blind, and now I can see!" ²⁶ "But what did he do?" they asked. "How did he heal you?" ²⁷ "Look!" the man exclaimed. "I told you once. Didn't you listen? Why do you want to hear it again? Do you want to become his disciples, too?" ²⁸ Then they cursed him and said, "You are his disciple, but we are disciples of Moses! ²⁹ We know God spoke to Moses, but we don't even know where this man comes from." ³⁰ "Why, that's very strange!" the man replied. "He healed my eyes, and yet you don't know where he comes from? ³¹ We know that God doesn't listen to sinners, but he is ready to hear those who worship him and do his will. ³² Ever since the world began, no one has been able to open the eyes of someone born blind. ³³ If this man were not from God, he couldn't have done it." ³⁴ "You were born a total sinner!" they answered. "Are you trying to teach us?" And they threw him out of the synagogue.

SPIRITUAL BLINDNESS

[35] When Jesus heard what had happened, he found the man and asked, "Do you believe in the Son of Man?" [36] The man answered, "Who is he, sir? I want to believe in him." [37] "You have seen him," Jesus said, "and he is speaking to you!" [38] "Yes, Lord, I believe!" the man said. And he worshiped Jesus. [39] Then Jesus told him, "I entered this world to render judgment—to give sight to the blind and to show those who think they see that they are blind." [40] Some Pharisees who were standing nearby heard him and asked, "Are you saying we're blind?" [41] "If you were blind, you wouldn't be guilty," Jesus replied. "But you remain guilty because you claim you can see.

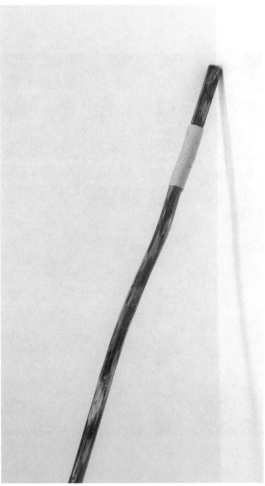

10

THE GOOD SHEPHERD AND HIS SHEEP

[1] "I tell you the truth, anyone who sneaks over the wall of a sheepfold, rather than going through the gate, must surely be a thief and a robber! [2] But the one who enters through the gate is the shepherd of the sheep. [3] The gatekeeper opens the gate for him, and the sheep recognize his voice and come to him. He calls his own sheep by name and leads them out. [4] After he has gathered his own flock, he walks ahead of them, and they follow him because they know his voice. [5] They won't follow a stranger; they will run from him because they don't know his voice." [6] Those who heard Jesus use this illustration didn't understand what he meant, [7] so he explained it to them: "I tell you the truth, I am the gate for the sheep. [8] All who came before me were thieves and robbers. But the true sheep did not listen to them. [9] Yes, I am the gate. Those who come in through me will be saved. They will come and go freely and will find good pastures. [10] The thief's purpose is to steal and kill and destroy. My purpose is to give them a rich and satisfying life. [11] I am the good shepherd. The good shepherd sacrifices his life for the sheep. [12] A hired hand will run when he sees a wolf coming. He will abandon the sheep because they don't belong to him and he isn't their shepherd. And so the wolf attacks them and scatters the flock. [13] The hired hand runs away because he's working only for the money and doesn't really care about the sheep. [14] I am the good shepherd; I know my own sheep, and they know me, [15] just as my Father knows me and I know the Father. So I sacrifice my life for the sheep. [16] I have other sheep, too, that are not in this sheepfold. I must bring them also. They will listen to my voice, and there will be one flock with one shepherd. [17] The Father loves me because I sacrifice my life so I may take it back again. [18] No one can take my life from me. I sacrifice it voluntarily. For I have the authority to lay it down when I want to and also to take it up again. For this is what my Father has commanded." [19] When he said these things, the people were again divided in their opinions about him. [20] Some said, "He's demon possessed and out of his mind. Why listen to a man like that?" [21] Others said, "This doesn't sound like a man possessed by a demon! Can a demon open the eyes of the blind?"

JESUS CLAIMS TO BE THE SON OF GOD

[22] It was now winter, and Jesus was in Jerusalem at the time of Hanukkah, the Festival of Dedication. [23] He was in the Temple, walking through the section known as Solomon's Colonnade. [24] The people surrounded him and asked, "How long are you going to keep us in suspense? If you are the Messiah, tell us plainly." [25] Jesus replied, "I have already told you, and you don't believe me. The proof is the work I do in my Father's name. [26] But you don't believe me because you are not my sheep. [27] My sheep listen to my voice; I know them, and they follow me. [28] I give them eternal life, and they will never perish. No one can snatch them away from me, [29] for my Father has given them to me, and he is more powerful than anyone else. No one can snatch them from the Father's hand. [30] The Father and I are one." [31] Once again the people picked up stones to kill him. [32] Jesus said, "At my Father's direction I have done many good works. For which one are you going to stone me?" [33] They replied, "We're stoning you not for any good work, but for blasphemy! You, a mere man, claim to be God." [34] Jesus replied, "It is written in your own Scriptures that God said to certain leaders of the people, 'I say, you are gods!' [35] And you know that the Scriptures cannot be altered. So if those people who received God's message were called 'gods,' [36] why do you call it blasphemy when I say, 'I am the Son of God'? After all, the Father set me apart and sent me into the world. [37] Don't believe me unless I carry out my Father's work. [38] But if I do his work, believe in the evidence of the miraculous works I have done, even if you don't believe me. Then you will know and understand that the Father is in me, and I am in the Father." [39] Once again they tried to arrest him, but he got away and left them. [40] He went beyond the Jordan River near the place where John was first baptizing and stayed there awhile. [41] And many followed him. "John didn't perform miraculous signs," they remarked to one another, "but everything he said about this man has come true." [42] And many who were there believed in Jesus.

JESUS CLAIMS TO BE THE SON OF GOD

JOHN 10:22-31

READ

1. Read John 10:22-31 slowly (aloud, if it's not intrusive to others).
2. Look at the photo on page 24.

REFLECT

1. Read the passage again, slowly.
2. Notice the confusion and frustration of the people around Jesus and their final response (v. 31).
3. Examine the photo on page 24 again.
4. Finally, read verses 27-29.
5. How do Jesus' words there address the mystery involved in our life with God?
6. What is your response to Jesus' statements in those verses? What, if anything, do you sense God inviting you to consider? To feel? To do?

RESPOND

1. Tell God how you feel about the mystery and journey of discovery in our life with God.
2. If you wish, ask for help recognizing God's voice.

REST

1. Read aloud verses 27-29 again.
2. Exhale.
3. Experiment with resting contentedly even when there is a lot you don't know or understand.
4. As you do so, position your body in whatever way expresses this: seated and head bowed, standing with arms and hands raised, kneeling on the floor, remaining in the position of the body in the photo.

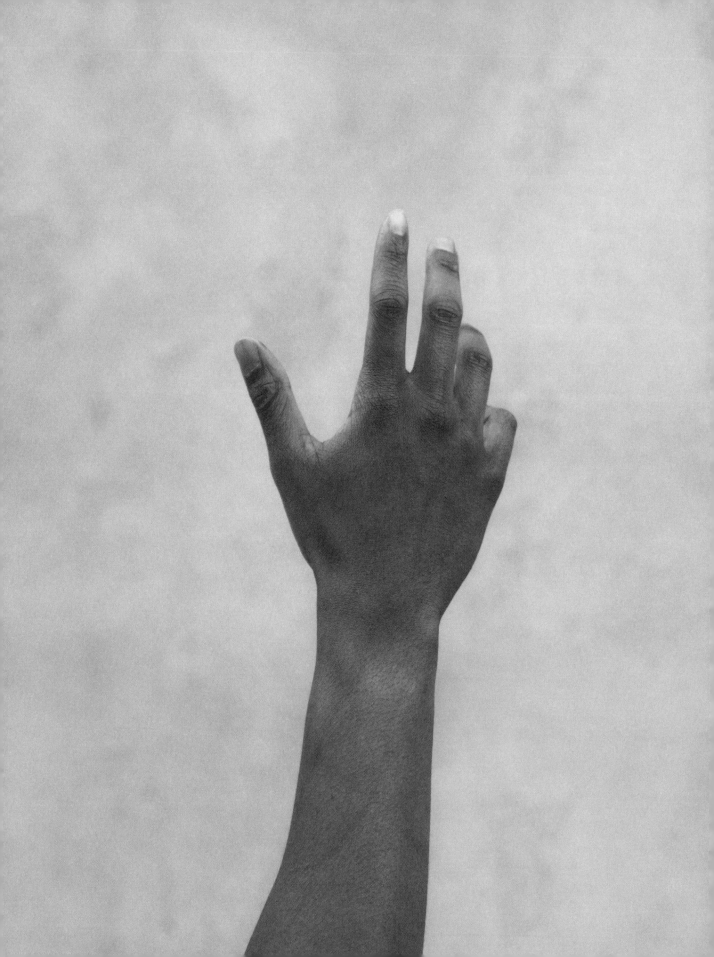

11

THE RAISING OF LAZARUS

¹ A man named Lazarus was sick. He lived in Bethany with his sisters, Mary and Martha. ² This is the Mary who later poured the expensive perfume on the Lord's feet and wiped them with her hair. Her brother, Lazarus, was sick. ³ So the two sisters sent a message to Jesus telling him, "Lord, your dear friend is very sick." ⁴ But when Jesus heard about it he said, "Lazarus's sickness will not end in death. No, it happened for the glory of God so that the Son of God will receive glory from this." ⁵ So although Jesus loved Martha, Mary, and Lazarus, ⁶ he stayed where he was for the next two days. ⁷ Finally, he said to his disciples, "Let's go back to Judea." ⁸ But his disciples objected. "Rabbi," they said, "only a few days ago the people in Judea were trying to stone you. Are you going there again?" ⁹ Jesus replied, "There are twelve hours of daylight every day. During the day people can walk safely. They can see because they have the light of this world. ¹⁰ But at night there is danger of stumbling because they have no light." ¹¹ Then he said, "Our friend Lazarus has fallen asleep, but now I will go and wake him up." ¹² The disciples said, "Lord, if he is sleeping, he will soon get better!" ¹³ They thought Jesus meant Lazarus was simply sleeping, but Jesus meant Lazarus had died. ¹⁴ So he told them plainly, "Lazarus is dead. ¹⁵ And for your sakes, I'm glad I wasn't there, for now you will really believe. Come, let's go see

him." [16] Thomas, nicknamed the Twin, said to his fellow disciples, "Let's go, too—and die with Jesus." [17] When Jesus arrived at Bethany, he was told that Lazarus had already been in his grave for four days. [18] Bethany was only a few miles down the road from Jerusalem, [19] and many of the people had come to console Martha and Mary in their loss. [20] When Martha got word that Jesus was coming, she went to meet him. But Mary stayed in the house. [21] Martha said to Jesus, "Lord, if only you had been here, my brother would not have died. [22] But even now I know that God will give you whatever you ask." [23] Jesus told her, "Your brother will rise again." [24] "Yes," Martha said, "he will rise when everyone else rises, at the last day." [25] Jesus told her, "I am the resurrection and the life. Anyone who believes in me will live, even after dying. [26] Everyone who lives in me and believes in me will never ever die. Do you believe this, Martha?" [27] "Yes, Lord," she told him. "I have always believed you

are the Messiah, the Son of God, the one who has come into the world from God." [28] Then she returned to Mary. She called Mary aside from the mourners and told her, "The Teacher is here and wants to see you." [29] So Mary immediately went to him. [30] Jesus had stayed outside the village, at the place where Martha met him. [31] When the people who were at the house consoling Mary saw her leave so hastily, they assumed she was going to Lazarus's grave to weep. So they followed her there. [32] When Mary arrived and saw Jesus, she fell at his feet and said, "Lord, if only you had been here, my brother would not have died." [33] When Jesus saw her weeping and saw the other people wailing with her, a deep anger welled up within him, and he was deeply troubled. [34] "Where have you put him?" he asked them. They told him, "Lord, come and see." [35] Then Jesus wept. [36] The people who were standing nearby said, "See how much he loved him!" [37] But some said, "This man healed a blind man. Couldn't he have kept Lazarus from dying?" [38] Jesus was still angry as he arrived at the tomb, a cave with a stone rolled across its entrance. [39] "Roll the stone aside," Jesus told them. But Martha, the dead man's sister, protested, "Lord, he has been dead for four days. The smell will be terrible." [40] Jesus responded, "Didn't I tell you that you would see God's glory if you believe?" [41] So they rolled the stone aside. Then Jesus looked up to heaven and said, "Father, thank you for hearing me. [42] You always hear me, but I said it out loud for the sake of all these people standing here, so that they will believe you sent me." [43] Then Jesus shouted, "Lazarus, come out!" [44] And the dead man came out, his hands and feet bound in graveclothes, his face wrapped in a headcloth. Jesus told them, "Unwrap him and let him go!"

THE PLOT TO KILL JESUS

[45] Many of the people who were with Mary believed in Jesus when they saw this happen. [46] But some went to the Pharisees and told them what Jesus had done. [47] Then the leading priests and Pharisees called the high council together. "What are we going to do?" they asked each other. "This man certainly performs many miraculous signs. [48] If we allow him to go on like this, soon everyone will believe in him. Then the Roman army will come and destroy both our Temple and our nation." [49] Caiaphas, who was high priest at that time, said, "You don't know what you're talking about! [50] You don't realize that it's better for you that one man should die for the people than for the whole nation to be destroyed." [51] He did not say this on his own; as high priest at that time he was led to prophesy that Jesus would die for the entire nation. [52] And not only for that nation, but to bring together and unite all the children of God scattered around the world. [53] So from that time on, the Jewish leaders began to plot Jesus' death. [54] As a result, Jesus stopped his public ministry among the people and left Jerusalem. He went to a place near the wilderness, to the village of Ephraim, and stayed there with his disciples. [55] It was now almost time for the Jewish Passover celebration, and many people from all over the country arrived in Jerusalem several days early so they could go through the purification ceremony before Passover began. [56] They kept looking for Jesus, but as they stood around in the Temple, they said to each other, "What do you think? He won't come for Passover, will he?" [57] Meanwhile, the leading priests and Pharisees had publicly ordered that anyone seeing Jesus must report it immediately so they could arrest him.

12

JESUS ANOINTED AT BETHANY

[1] Six days before the Passover celebration began, Jesus arrived in Bethany, the home of Lazarus—the man he had raised from the dead. [2] A dinner was prepared in Jesus' honor. Martha served, and Lazarus was among those who ate with him. [3] Then Mary took a twelve-ounce jar of expensive perfume made from essence of nard, and she anointed Jesus' feet with it, wiping his feet with her hair. The house was filled with the fragrance. [4] But Judas Iscariot, the disciple who would soon betray him, said, [5] "That perfume was worth a year's wages. It should have been sold and the money given to the poor." [6] Not that he cared for the poor—he was a thief, and since he was in charge of the disciples' money, he often stole some for himself. [7] Jesus replied, "Leave her alone. She did this in preparation for my burial. [8] You will always have the poor among you, but you will not always have me." [9] When all the people heard of Jesus' arrival, they flocked to see him and also to see Lazarus, the man Jesus had raised from the dead. [10] Then the leading priests decided to kill Lazarus, too, [11] for it was because of him that many of the people had deserted them and believed in Jesus.

JESUS' TRIUMPHANT ENTRY

[12] The next day, the news that Jesus was on the way to Jerusalem swept through the city. A large crowd of Passover visitors [13] took palm branches and went down the road to meet him. They shouted, "Praise God! Blessings on the one who comes in the name of the LORD! Hail to the King of Israel!" [14] Jesus found a young donkey and rode on it, fulfilling the prophecy that said: [15] "Don't be afraid, people of Jerusalem. Look, your King is coming, riding on a donkey's colt." [16] His disciples didn't understand at the time that this was a fulfillment of prophecy. But after Jesus entered into his glory, they remembered what had happened and realized that these things had been written about him. [17] Many in the crowd had seen Jesus call Lazarus from the tomb, raising him from the dead, and they were telling others about it. [18] That was the reason so many went out to meet him—because they had heard about this miraculous sign. [19] Then the Pharisees said to each other, "There's nothing we can do. Look, everyone has gone after him!"

JESUS PREDICTS HIS DEATH

[20] Some Greeks who had come to Jerusalem for the Passover celebration [21] paid a visit to Philip, who was from Bethsaida in Galilee. They said, "Sir, we want to meet Jesus." [22] Philip told Andrew about it, and they went together to ask Jesus. [23] Jesus replied, "Now the time has come for the Son of Man to enter into his glory. [24] I tell you the truth, unless a kernel of wheat is planted in the soil and dies, it remains alone. But its death will produce many new kernels—a plentiful harvest of new lives. [25] Those who love their life in this world will lose it. Those who care nothing for their life in this world will keep it for eternity. [26] Anyone who wants to serve me must follow me, because my servants must be where I am. And the Father will honor anyone who serves me. [27] Now my soul is deeply troubled. Should I pray, 'Father, save me from this hour'? But this is the very reason I came! [28] Father, bring glory to your name." Then a voice spoke from heaven, saying, "I have already brought glory to my name, and I will do so again." [29] When the crowd heard the voice, some thought it was thunder, while others declared an angel had spoken to him. [30] Then Jesus told them, "The voice was for your benefit, not mine. [31] The time for judging this world has come, when Satan, the ruler of this world, will be cast out. [32] And when I am lifted up from the earth, I will draw everyone to myself." [33] He said this to indicate how he was going to die. [34] The crowd responded, "We understood from Scripture that the Messiah would live forever. How can you say the Son of Man will die? Just who is this Son of Man, anyway?" [35] Jesus replied, "My light will shine for you just a little longer. Walk in the light while you can, so the darkness will not overtake you. Those who walk in the darkness cannot see where they are going. [36] Put your trust in the light while there is still time; then you will become children of the light." After saying these things, Jesus went away and was hidden from them.

THE UNBELIEF OF THE PEOPLE

[37] But despite all the miraculous signs Jesus had done, most of the people still did not believe in him. [38] This is exactly what Isaiah the prophet had predicted: "LORD, who has believed our message? To whom has the LORD revealed his powerful arm?" [39] But the people couldn't believe, for as Isaiah also said, [40] "The LORD has blinded their eyes and hardened their hearts—so that their eyes cannot see, and their hearts cannot understand, and they cannot turn to me and have me heal them." [41] Isaiah was referring to Jesus when he said this, because he saw the future and spoke of the Messiah's glory. [42] Many people did believe in him, however, including some of the Jewish leaders. But they wouldn't admit it for fear that the Pharisees would expel them from the synagogue. [43] For they loved human praise more than the praise of God. [44] Jesus shouted to the crowds, "If you trust me, you are trusting not only me, but also God who sent me. [45] For when you see me, you are seeing the one who sent me. [46] I have come as a light to shine in this dark world, so that all who put their trust in me will no longer remain in the dark. [47] I will not judge those who hear me but don't obey me, for I have come to save the world and not to judge it. [48] But all who reject me and my message will be judged on the day of judgment by the truth I have spoken. [49] I don't speak on my own authority. The Father who sent me has commanded me what to say and how to say it. [50] And I know his commands lead to eternal life; so I say whatever the Father tells me to say."

JESUS PREDICTS HIS DEATH

JOHN 12:20-26

READ

1. Read John 12:20-26 slowly (aloud, if it's not intrusive to others).
2. Look at the photo on page 63. How might these boardwalk doorways (marking the beginning and ending of a salt marsh) relate to Jesus' prediction of his death?
3. Pause.

REFLECT

1. Read the passage and consider Jesus' dilemma in trying to explain that he would pass through death and come out the other side.
2. No one had ever seen anything like this.
3. Read the passage again and consider the listeners' dilemma as they tried to understand how new life could come out of death.
4. Have you experienced times of dying to self(ishness) and finding new life (vv. 24-25)?
5. Read again slowly and notice what stands out to you. What words or phrases resonate with you?
6. Ask God why that might be.
7. What, if anything, do you sense God inviting you to consider? To feel? To do?

RESPOND

1. Imagine yourself in the photo, keeping in mind any difficult or challenging doorways you have passed through.
2. Tell God where you would be.
3. Ask for help for anything you need to die to and come back to life to.

REST

1. Exhale.
2. Soak in the freedom that comes from dying to self and not trying to manage the outcomes of your life all on your own.
3. Even if that's not where you are at this time, try imagining that and feeling that freedom.

13

JESUS WASHES HIS DISCIPLES' FEET

[1] Before the Passover celebration, Jesus knew that his hour had come to leave this world and return to his Father. He had loved his disciples during his ministry on earth, and now he loved them to the very end. [2] It was time for supper, and the devil had already prompted Judas, son of Simon Iscariot, to betray Jesus. [3] Jesus knew that the Father had given him authority over everything and that he had come from God and would return to God. [4] So he got up from the table, took off his robe, wrapped a towel around his waist, [5] and poured water into a basin. Then he began to wash the disciples' feet, drying them with the towel he had around him. [6] When Jesus came to Simon Peter, Peter said to him, "Lord, are you going to wash my feet?" [7] Jesus replied, "You don't understand now what I am doing, but someday you will." [8] "No," Peter protested, "you will never ever wash my feet!" Jesus replied, "Unless I wash you, you won't belong to me." [9] Simon Peter exclaimed, "Then wash my hands and head as well, Lord, not just my feet!" [10] Jesus replied, "A person who has bathed all over does not need to wash, except for the feet, to be entirely clean. And you disciples are clean, but not all of you." [11] For Jesus knew who would betray him. That is what he meant when he said, "Not all of you are clean." [12] After washing their feet, he put on his robe again and sat down and asked, "Do you understand what I was doing? [13] You call me 'Teacher' and 'Lord,' and you are right, because that's what I am. [14] And since I, your Lord and Teacher, have washed your feet, you ought to wash each other's feet. [15] I have given you an example to follow. Do as I have done to you. [16] I tell you the truth, slaves are not greater than their master. Nor is the messenger more important than the one who sends the message. [17] Now that you know these things, God will bless you for doing them."

JESUS PREDICTS HIS BETRAYAL

[18] "I am not saying these things to all of you; I know the ones I have chosen. But this fulfills the Scripture that says, 'The one who eats my food has turned against me.' [19] I tell you this beforehand, so that when it happens you will believe that I am the Messiah. [20] I tell you the truth, anyone who welcomes my messenger is welcoming me, and anyone who welcomes me is welcoming the Father who sent me."

[21] Now Jesus was deeply troubled, and he exclaimed, "I tell you the truth, one of you will betray me!" [22] The disciples looked at each other, wondering whom he could mean. [23] The disciple Jesus loved was sitting next to Jesus at the table. [24] Simon Peter motioned to him to ask, "Who's he talking about?" [25] So that disciple leaned over to Jesus and asked, "Lord, who is it?" [26] Jesus responded, "It is the one to whom I give the bread I dip in the bowl." And when he had dipped it, he gave it to Judas, son of Simon Iscariot. [27] When Judas had eaten the bread, Satan entered into him. Then Jesus told him, "Hurry and do what you're going to do." [28] None of the others at the table knew what Jesus meant. [29] Since Judas was their treasurer, some thought Jesus was telling him to go and pay for the food or to give some money to the poor. [30] So Judas left at once, going out into the night.

JESUS PREDICTS PETER'S DENIAL

[31] As soon as Judas left the room, Jesus said, "The time has come for the Son of Man to enter into his glory, and God will be glorified because of him. [32] And since God receives glory because of the Son, he will give his own glory to the Son, and he will do so at once. [33] Dear children, I will be with you only a little longer. And as I told the Jewish leaders, you will search for me, but you can't come where I am going. [34] So now I am giving you a new commandment: Love each other. Just as I have loved you, you should love each other. [35] Your love for one another will prove to the world that you are my disciples." [36] Simon Peter asked, "Lord, where are you going?" And Jesus replied, "You can't go with me now, but you will follow me later." [37] "But why can't I come now, Lord?" he asked. "I'm ready to die for you." [38] Jesus answered, "Die for me? I tell you the truth, Peter—before the rooster crows tomorrow morning, you will deny three times that you even know me."

JESUS, THE WAY TO THE FATHER

JOHN 14:1-12

READ

1. Before reading the passage, put yourself in the place of Jesus. This is your final communication to these followers you love.
2. Read John 14:1-12 (aloud, if it's not intrusive to others) as if you were Jesus speaking strategically to the disciples.
3. Look at the photo on page 68.
4. Pause.

REFLECT

1. Read again, slowly.
2. Notice the details of the photo: the door is open enough to see a bit of light, perhaps the hint of things to come. It's rather mysterious, as if you're peeking behind a curtain.
3. Is there a space in your life where this minimal yet clearly highlighted understanding is your reality?
4. If not, is there a circumstance in which you would like for that to be true?
5. Read the passage again and notice what stands out to you.
6. What words or phrases resonate with you?

7. Ask God why that might be.
8. What, if anything, do you sense God inviting you to consider? To feel? To do?

RESPOND

1. Rephrase verses 11 and 12 in your own words as a prayer, perhaps something like this:

   Jesus, I believe that you are in the Father and the Father is in you. These words in John are not just yours but also the Father's. I trust that you and the Father are one. I'm able to trust because of the works I see that are recorded in the Gospels.

2. Then state a way that you would like to trust Jesus more—a situation, an illness, a feeling, a task.

REST

1. Read aloud verses 11-12.
2. Exhale.
3. Soak in the invitation from Jesus to trust him—that God works in him, including God's goodness and God's power.

14

JESUS, THE WAY TO THE FATHER

[1] "Don't let your hearts be troubled. Trust in God, and trust also in me. [2] There is more than enough room in my Father's home. If this were not so, would I have told you that I am going to prepare a place for you? [3] When everything is ready, I will come and get you, so that you will always be with me where I am. [4] And you know the way to where I am going." [5] "No, we don't know, Lord," Thomas said. "We have no idea where you are going, so how can we know the way?" [6] Jesus told him, "I am the way, the truth, and the life. No one can come to the Father except through me. [7] If you had really known me, you would know who my Father is. From now on, you do know him and have seen him!" [8] Philip said, "Lord, show us the Father, and we will be satisfied." [9] Jesus replied, "Have I been with you all this time, Philip, and yet you still don't know who I am? Anyone who has seen me has seen the Father! So why are you asking me to show him to you? [10] Don't you believe that I am in the Father and the Father is in me? The words I speak are not my own, but my Father who lives in me does his work through me. [11] Just believe that I am in the Father and the Father is in me. Or at least believe because of the work you have seen me do. [12] I tell you the truth, anyone who believes in me will do the same works I have done, and even greater works, because I am going to be with the Father. [13] You can ask for anything in my name, and I will do it, so that the Son can bring glory to the Father. [14] Yes, ask me for anything in my name, and I will do it!"

JESUS PROMISES THE HOLY SPIRIT

[15] "If you love me, obey my commandments. [16] And I will ask the Father, and he will give you another Advocate, who will never leave you. [17] He is the Holy Spirit, who leads into all truth. The world cannot receive him, because it isn't looking for him and doesn't recognize him. But you know him, because he lives with you now and later will be in you. [18] No, I will not abandon you as orphans—I will come to you. [19] Soon the world will no longer see me, but you will see me. Since I live, you also will live. [20] When I am raised to life again, you will know that I am in my Father, and you are in me, and I am in you. [21] Those who accept my commandments and obey them are the ones who love me. And because they love me, my Father will love them. And I will love them and reveal myself to each of them." [22] Judas (not Judas Iscariot, but the other disciple with that name) said to him, "Lord, why are you going to reveal yourself only to us and not to the world at large?" [23] Jesus replied, "All who love me will do what I say. My Father will love them, and we will come and make

our home with each of them. ²⁴ Anyone who doesn't love me will not obey me. And remember, my words are not my own. What I am telling you is from the Father who sent me. ²⁵ I am telling you these things now while I am still with you. ²⁶ But when the Father sends the Advocate as my representative—that is, the Holy Spirit—he will teach you everything and will remind you of everything I have told you. ²⁷ I am leaving you with a gift—peace of mind and heart. And the peace I give is a gift the world cannot give. So don't be troubled or afraid. ²⁸ Remember what I told you: I am going away, but I will come back to you again. If you really loved me, you would be happy that I am going to the Father, who is greater than I am. ²⁹ I have told you these things before they happen so that when they do happen, you will believe. ³⁰ I don't have much more time to talk to you, because the ruler of this world approaches. He has no power over me, 31 but I will do what the Father requires of me, so that the world will know that I love the Father. Come, let's be going."

15

JESUS, THE TRUE VINE

[1] "I am the true grapevine, and my Father is the gardener. [2] He cuts off every branch of mine that doesn't produce fruit, and he prunes the branches that do bear fruit so they will produce even more. [3] You have already been pruned and purified by the message I have given you. [4] Remain in me, and I will remain in you. For a branch cannot produce fruit if it is severed from the vine, and you cannot be fruitful unless you remain in me. [5] Yes, I am the vine; you are the branches. Those who remain in me, and I in them, will produce much fruit. For apart from me you can do nothing. [6] Anyone who does not remain in me is thrown away like a useless branch and withers. Such branches are gathered into a pile to be burned. [7] But if you remain in me and my words remain in you, you may ask for anything you want, and it will be granted! [8] When you produce much fruit, you are my true disciples. This brings great glory to my Father. [9] I have loved you even as the Father has loved me. Remain in my love. [10] When you obey my commandments, you remain in my love, just as I obey my Father's commandments and remain in his love. [11] I have told you these things so that you will be filled with my joy. Yes, your joy will overflow! [12] This is my commandment: Love each other in the same way I have loved you. [13] There is no greater love than to lay down one's life for one's friends. [14] You are my friends if you do what I command. [15] I no longer call you slaves, because a master doesn't confide in his slaves. Now you are my friends, since I have told you everything the Father told me. [16] You didn't choose me. I chose you. I appointed you to go and produce lasting fruit, so that the Father will give you whatever you ask for, using my name. [17] This is my command: Love each other.

THE WORLD'S HATRED

[18] "If the world hates you, remember that it hated me first. [19] The world would love you as one of its own if you belonged to it, but you are no longer part of the world. I chose you to come out of the world, so it hates you. [20] Do you remember what I told you? 'A slave is not greater than the master.' Since they persecuted me, naturally they will persecute you. And if they had listened to me, they would listen to you. [21] They will do all this to you because of me, for they have rejected the one who sent me. [22] They would not be guilty if I had not come and spoken to them. But now they have no excuse for their sin. [23] Anyone who hates me also hates my Father. [24] If I hadn't done such miraculous signs among them that no one else could do, they would not be guilty. But as it is, they have seen everything I did, yet they still hate me and my Father. [25] This fulfills what is written in their Scriptures: 'They hated me without cause.' [26] But I will send you the Advocate—the Spirit of truth. He will come to you from the Father and will testify all about me. [27] And you must also testify about me because you have been with me from the beginning of my ministry."

16

¹ "I have told you these things so that you won't abandon your faith. ² For you will be expelled from the synagogues, and the time is coming when those who kill you will think they are doing a holy service for God. ³ This is because they have never known the Father or me. ⁴ Yes, I'm telling you these things now, so that when they happen, you will remember my warning. I didn't tell you earlier because I was going to be with you for a while longer.

THE WORK OF THE HOLY SPIRIT

⁵ "But now I am going away to the one who sent me, and not one of you is asking where I am going. ⁶ Instead, you grieve because of what I've told you. ⁷ But in fact, it is best for you that I go away, because if I don't, the Advocate won't come. If I do go away, then I will send him to you. ⁸ And when he comes, he will convict the world of its sin, and of God's righteousness, and of the coming judgment. ⁹ The world's sin is that it refuses to believe in me. ¹⁰ Righteousness is available because I go to the Father, and you will see me no more. ¹¹ Judgment will come because the ruler of this world has already been judged. ¹² There is so much more I want to tell you, but you can't bear it now. ¹³ When the Spirit of truth comes, he will guide you into all truth. He will not speak on his own but will tell you what he has heard. He will tell you about the future. ¹⁴ He will bring me glory by telling you whatever he receives from me. ¹⁵ All that belongs to the Father is mine; this is why I said, 'The Spirit will tell you whatever he receives from me.'

SADNESS WILL BE TURNED TO JOY

¹⁶ "In a little while you won't see me anymore. But a little while after that, you will see me again." ¹⁷ Some of the disciples asked each other, "What does he mean when he says, 'In a little while you won't see me,

but then you will see me,' and 'I am going to the Father'? [18] And what does he mean by 'a little while'? We don't understand." [19] Jesus realized they wanted to ask him about it, so he said, "Are you asking yourselves what I meant? I said in a little while you won't see me, but a little while after that you will see me again. [20] I tell you the truth, you will weep and mourn over what is going to happen to me, but the world will rejoice. You will grieve, but your grief will suddenly turn to wonderful joy. [21] It will be like a woman suffering the pains of labor. When her child is born, her anguish gives way to joy because she has brought a new baby into the world. [22] So you have sorrow now, but I will see you again; then you will rejoice, and no one can rob you of that joy. [23] At that time you won't need to ask me for anything. I tell you the truth, you will ask the Father directly, and he will grant your request because you use my name. [24] You haven't done this before. Ask, using my name, and you will receive, and you will have abundant joy. [25] I have spoken of these matters in figures of speech, but soon I will stop speaking figuratively and will tell you plainly all about the Father. [26] Then you will ask in my name. I'm not saying I will ask the Father on your behalf, [27] for the Father himself loves you dearly because you love me and believe that I came from God. [28] Yes, I came from the Father into the world, and now I will leave the world and return to the Father." [29] Then his disciples said, "At last you are speaking plainly and not figuratively. [30] Now we understand that you know everything, and there's no need to question you. From this we believe that you came from God." [31] Jesus asked, "Do you finally believe? [32] But the time is coming—indeed it's here now—when you will be scattered, each one going his own way, leaving me alone. Yet I am not alone because the Father is with me. [33] I have told you all this so that you may have peace in me. Here on earth you will have many trials and sorrows. But take heart, because I have overcome the world."

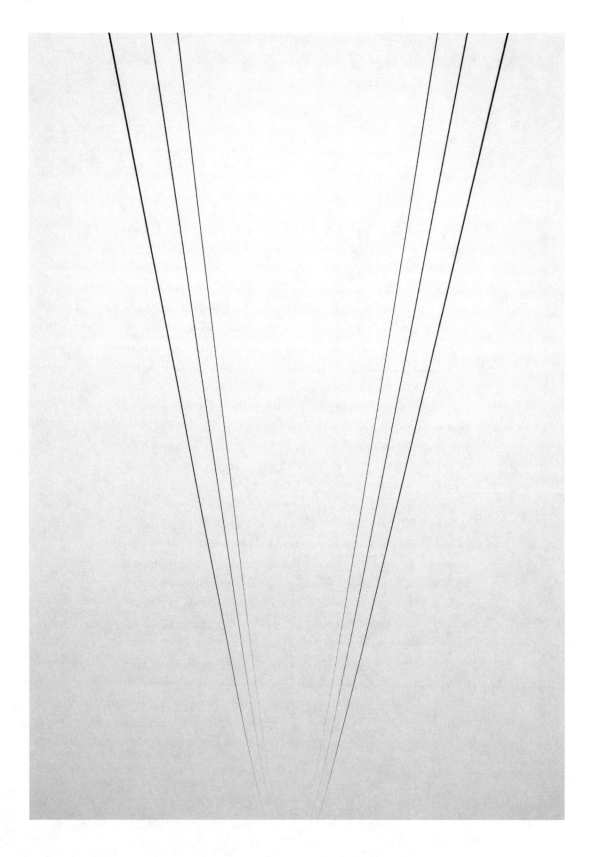

17

THE PRAYER OF JESUS

¹ After saying all these things, Jesus looked up to heaven and said, "Father, the hour has come. Glorify your Son so he can give glory back to you. ² For you have given him authority over everyone. He gives eternal life to each one you have given him. ³ And this is the way to have eternal life—to know you, the only true God, and Jesus Christ, the one you sent to earth. ⁴ I brought glory to you here on earth by completing the work you gave me to do. ⁵ Now, Father, bring me into the glory we shared before the world began. ⁶ "I have revealed you to the ones you gave me from this world. They were always yours. You gave them to me, and they have kept your word. ⁷ Now they know that everything I have is a gift from you, ⁸ for I have passed on to them the message you gave me. They accepted it and know that I came from you, and they believe you sent me. ⁹ My prayer is not for the world, but for those you have given me, because they belong to you. ¹⁰ All who are mine belong to you, and you have given them to me, so they bring me glory. ¹¹ Now I am departing from the world; they are staying in this world, but I am coming to you. Holy Father, you have given me your name; now protect them by the power of your name so that they will be united just as we are. ¹² During my time here, I protected them by the power of the name you gave me. I guarded them so that not one was lost, except the one headed for destruction, as the Scriptures foretold. ¹³ "Now I am coming to you. I told them

many things while I was with them in this world so they would be filled with my joy. ¹⁴ I have given them your word. And the world hates them because they do not belong to the world, just as I do not belong to the world. ¹⁵ I'm not asking you to take them out of the world, but to keep them safe from the evil one. ¹⁶ They do not belong to this world any more than I do. ¹⁷ Make them holy by your truth; teach them your word, which is truth. ¹⁸ Just as you sent me into the world, I am sending them into the world. ¹⁹ And I give myself as a holy sacrifice for them so they can be made holy by your truth. ²⁰ I am praying not only for these disciples but also for all who will ever believe in me through their message. ²¹ I pray that they will all be one, just as you and I are one—as you are in me, Father, and I am in you. And may they be in us so that the world will believe you sent me. ²² I have given them the glory you gave me, so they may be one as we are one. ²³ I am in them and you are in me. May they experience such perfect unity that the world will know that you sent me and that you love them as much as you love me. ²⁴ Father, I want these whom you have given me to be with me where I am. Then they can see all the glory you gave me because you loved me even before the world began! ²⁵ O righteous Father, the world doesn't know you, but I do; and these disciples know you sent me. ²⁶ I have revealed you to them, and I will continue to do so. Then your love for me will be in them, and I will be in them."

THE PRAYER OF JESUS

JOHN 17:21-23

READ

1. Read John 17:21-23 slowly (aloud, if it's not intrusive to others).
2. Look at the photo on page 76.
3. Pause.

REFLECT

1. Stretch your thumb and forefinger from the lines farthest apart at the top of the photo.
2. Hold your fingers in that position and then set them at the bottom of the photo.
3. Notice how much closer the lines are at the bottom from the way they are at the top.
4. Leave your hand in this position and reread the passage.
5. Read the text aloud, if possible, once again putting yourself in the place of Jesus praying this prayer. How do you think he may have felt when he prayed this?

6. Read the passage again and notice what comes to you.
7. What, if anything, do you sense God inviting you to consider? To feel? To do?

RESPOND

1. Fold your hands in prayer, as children often do. Press your palms together until they touch. Notice the closeness of your hands.
2. Ask for oneness in Christ for people or groups who don't seem to experience oneness in the church.
3. After each request, press your palms together, joining them together.

REST

1. Soak in the knowledge that oneness comes through people following the Spirit.
2. Rest in gratefulness that the Spirit does this work well.

18

JESUS IS BETRAYED AND ARRESTED

[1] After saying these things, Jesus crossed the Kidron Valley with his disciples and entered a grove of olive trees. [2] Judas, the betrayer, knew this place, because Jesus had often gone there with his disciples. [3] The leading priests and Pharisees had given Judas a contingent of Roman soldiers and Temple guards to accompany him. Now with blazing torches, lanterns, and weapons, they arrived at the olive grove. [4] Jesus fully realized all that was going to happen to him, so he stepped forward to meet them. "Who are you looking for?" he asked. [5] "Jesus the Nazarene," they replied. "I AM he," Jesus said. (Judas, who betrayed him, was standing with them.) [6] As Jesus said "I AM he," they all drew back and fell to the ground! [7] Once more he asked them, "Who are you looking for?" And again they replied, "Jesus the Nazarene." [8] "I told you that I AM he," Jesus said. "And since I am the one you want, let these others go." [9] He did this to fulfill his own statement: "I did not lose a single one of those you have given me." [10] Then Simon Peter drew a sword and slashed off the right ear of Malchus, the high priest's slave. [11] But Jesus said to Peter, "Put your sword back into its sheath. Shall I not drink from the cup of suffering the Father has given me?"

JESUS AT THE HIGH PRIEST'S HOUSE

[12] So the soldiers, their commanding officer, and the Temple guards arrested Jesus and tied him up. [13] First they took him to Annas, since he was the father-in-law of Caiaphas, the high priest at that time. [14] Caiaphas was the one who had told the other Jewish leaders, "It's better that one man should die for the people."

PETER'S FIRST DENIAL

[15] Simon Peter followed Jesus, as did another of the disciples. That other disciple was acquainted with the high priest, so he was allowed to enter the high priest's courtyard with Jesus. [16] Peter had to stay outside the gate. Then the disciple who knew the high priest spoke to the woman watching at the gate, and she let Peter in. [17] The woman asked Peter, "You're not one of that man's disciples, are you?" "No," he said, "I am not."[18] Because it was cold, the household servants and the guards had made a charcoal fire. They stood around it, warming themselves, and Peter stood with them, warming himself.

THE HIGH PRIEST QUESTIONS JESUS

[19] Inside, the high priest began asking Jesus about his followers and what he had been teaching them. [20] Jesus replied, "Everyone knows what I teach. I have preached regularly in the synagogues and the Temple, where the people gather. I have not spoken in secret. [21] Why are you asking me this question? Ask those who heard me. They know what I said." [22] Then one of the Temple guards standing nearby slapped Jesus across the face. "Is that the way to answer the high priest?" he demanded. [23] Jesus replied, "If I said anything wrong, you must prove it. But if I'm speaking the truth, why are you beating me?" [24] Then Annas bound Jesus and sent him to Caiaphas, the high priest.

PETER'S SECOND AND THIRD DENIALS

[25] Meanwhile, as Simon Peter was standing by the fire warming himself, they asked him again, "You're not one of his disciples, are you?" He denied it, saying, "No, I am not." [26] But one of the household slaves of the high priest, a relative of the man whose ear Peter had cut off, asked, "Didn't I see you out there in the olive grove with Jesus?" [27] Again Peter denied it. And immediately a rooster crowed.

JESUS' TRIAL BEFORE PILATE

[28] Jesus' trial before Caiaphas ended in the early hours of the morning. Then he was taken to the headquarters of the Roman governor. His accusers didn't go inside because it would defile them, and they wouldn't be allowed to celebrate the Passover. [29] So Pilate, the governor, went out to them and asked, "What is your charge against this man?" [30] "We wouldn't have handed him over to you if he weren't a criminal!" they retorted. [31] "Then take him away and judge him by your own law," Pilate told them. "Only the Romans are permitted to execute someone," the Jewish leaders replied. [32] (This fulfilled Jesus' prediction about the way he would die.) [33] Then Pilate went back into his headquarters and called for Jesus to be brought to him. "Are you the king of the Jews?" he asked him. [34] Jesus replied, "Is this your own question, or did others tell you about me?" [35] "Am I a Jew?" Pilate retorted. "Your own people and their leading priests brought you to me for trial. Why? What have you done?" [36] Jesus answered, "My Kingdom is not an earthly kingdom. If it were, my followers would fight to keep me from being handed over to the Jewish leaders. But my Kingdom is not of this world." [37] Pilate said, "So you are a king?" Jesus responded, "You say I am a king. Actually, I was born and came into the world to testify to the truth. All who love the truth recognize that what I say is true." [38] "What is truth?" Pilate asked. Then he went out again to the people and told them, "He is not guilty of any crime. [39] But you have a custom of asking me to release one prisoner each year at Passover. Would you like me to release this 'King of the Jews'?" [40] But they shouted back, "No! Not this man. We want Barabbas!" (Barabbas was a revolutionary.)

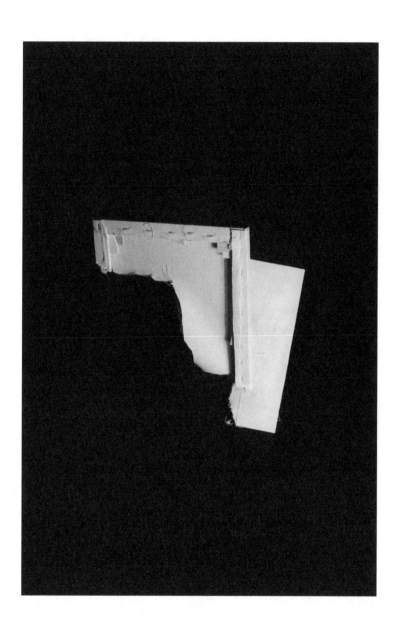

19

JESUS SENTENCED TO DEATH

[1] Then Pilate had Jesus flogged with a lead-tipped whip. [2] The soldiers wove a crown of thorns and put it on his head, and they put a purple robe on him. [3] "Hail! King of the Jews!" they mocked, as they slapped him across the face. [4] Pilate went outside again and said to the people, "I am going to bring him out to you now, but understand clearly that I find him not guilty." [5] Then Jesus came out wearing the crown of thorns and the purple robe. And Pilate said, "Look, here is the man!" [6] When they saw him, the leading priests and Temple guards began shouting, "Crucify him! Crucify him!" "Take him yourselves and crucify him," Pilate said. "I find him not guilty." [7] The Jewish leaders replied, "By our law he ought to die because he called himself the Son of God." [8] When Pilate heard this, he was more frightened than ever. [9] He took Jesus back into the headquarters again and asked him, "Where are you from?" But Jesus gave no answer. [10] "Why don't you talk to me?" Pilate demanded. "Don't you realize that I have the power to release you or crucify you?" [11] Then Jesus said, "You would have no power over me at all unless it were given to you from above. So the one who handed me over to you has the greater sin." [12] Then Pilate tried to release him, but the Jewish leaders shouted, "If you release this man, you are no 'friend of Caesar.' Anyone who declares himself a king is a rebel against Caesar." [13] When they said this, Pilate brought Jesus out to them again. Then Pilate sat down on the judgment seat on the platform that is called the Stone Pavement (in Hebrew, Gabbatha). [14] It was now about noon on the day of preparation for the Passover. And Pilate said to the people, "Look, here is your king!" [15] "Away with him," they yelled. "Away with him! Crucify him!" "What? Crucify your king?" Pilate asked. "We have no king but Caesar," the leading priests shouted back. [16] Then Pilate turned Jesus over to them to be crucified.

THE CRUCIFIXION

So they took Jesus away. [17] Carrying the cross by himself, he went to the place called Place of the Skull (in Hebrew, Golgotha). [18] There they nailed him to the cross. Two others were crucified with him, one on either side, with Jesus between them. [19] And Pilate posted a sign on the cross that read, "Jesus of Nazareth, the King of the Jews." [20] The place where Jesus was crucified was near the city, and the sign was written in Hebrew, Latin, and Greek, so that many people could read it. [21] Then the leading priests objected and said to Pilate, "Change it from 'The King of the Jews' to 'He said, I am King of the Jews.'" [22] Pilate replied, "No, what I have written, I have written." [23] When the soldiers had crucified Jesus, they divided his clothes among the four of them. They also took his robe, but it was seamless, woven in one piece from top to bottom. [24] So they said, "Rather than tearing it apart, let's throw dice for it." This fulfilled the Scripture that says, "They divided my garments among themselves and threw dice for my clothing." So that is what they did. [25] Standing near the cross were Jesus' mother, and his mother's sister, Mary (the wife of Clopas), and Mary Magdalene. [26] When Jesus saw his mother standing there beside the disciple he loved, he said to her, "Dear woman, here is your son." [27] And he said to this disciple, "Here is your mother." And from then on this disciple took her into his home.

THE DEATH OF JESUS

[28] Jesus knew that his mission was now finished, and to fulfill Scripture he said, "I am thirsty." [29] A jar of sour wine was sitting there, so they soaked a sponge in it, put it on a hyssop branch, and held it up to his

lips. [30] When Jesus had tasted it, he said, "It is finished!" Then he bowed his head and gave up his spirit. [31] It was the day of preparation, and the Jewish leaders didn't want the bodies hanging there the next day, which was the Sabbath (and a very special Sabbath, because it was Passover week). So they asked Pilate to hasten their deaths by ordering that their legs be broken. Then their bodies could be taken down. [32] So the soldiers came and broke the legs of the two men crucified with Jesus. [33] But when they came to Jesus, they saw that he was already dead, so they didn't break his legs. [34] One of the soldiers, however, pierced his side with a spear, and immediately blood and water flowed out. [35] (This report is from an eyewitness giving an accurate account. He speaks the truth so that you also may continue to believe.) [36] These things happened in fulfillment of the Scriptures that say, "Not one of his bones will be broken," [37] and "They will look on the one they pierced."

THE BURIAL OF JESUS

[38] Afterward Joseph of Arimathea, who had been a secret disciple of Jesus (because he feared the Jewish leaders), asked Pilate for permission to take down Jesus' body. When Pilate gave permission, Joseph came and took the body away. [39] With him came Nicodemus, the man who had come to Jesus at night. He brought about seventy-five pounds of perfumed ointment made from myrrh and aloes. [40] Following Jewish burial custom, they wrapped Jesus' body with the spices in long sheets of linen cloth. [41] The place of crucifixion was near a garden, where there was a new tomb, never used before. [42] And so, because it was the day of preparation for the Jewish Passover and since the tomb was close at hand, they laid Jesus there.

20

THE RESURRECTION

[1] Early on Sunday morning, while it was still dark, Mary Magdalene came to the tomb and found that the stone had been rolled away from the entrance. [2] She ran and found Simon Peter and the other disciple, the one whom Jesus loved. She said, "They have taken the Lord's body out of the tomb, and we don't know where they have put him!" [3] Peter and the other disciple started out for the tomb. [4] They were both running, but the other disciple outran Peter and reached the tomb first. [5] He stooped and looked in and saw the linen wrappings lying there, but he didn't go in. [6] Then Simon Peter arrived and went inside. He also noticed the linen wrappings lying there, [7] while the cloth that had covered Jesus' head was folded up and lying apart from the other wrappings. [8] Then the disciple who had reached the tomb first also went in, and he saw and believed— [9] for until then they still hadn't understood the Scriptures that said Jesus must rise from the dead. [10] Then they went home.

JESUS APPEARS TO MARY MAGDALENE

[11] Mary was standing outside the tomb crying, and as she wept, she stooped and looked in. [12] She saw two white-robed angels, one sitting at the head and the other at the foot of the place where the body of Jesus had been lying. [13] "Dear woman, why are you crying?" the angels asked her. "Because they have taken away my Lord," she replied, "and I don't know where they have put him." [14] She turned to leave and saw someone standing there. It was Jesus, but she didn't recognize him. [15] "Dear woman, why are you crying?" Jesus asked her. "Who are you

looking for?" She thought he was the gardener. "Sir," she said, "if you have taken him away, tell me where you have put him, and I will go and get him." [16] "Mary!" Jesus said. She turned to him and cried out, "Rabboni!" (which is Hebrew for "Teacher"). [17] "Don't cling to me," Jesus said, "for I haven't yet ascended to the Father. But go find my brothers and tell them, 'I am ascending to my Father and your Father, to my God and your God.'" [18] Mary Magdalene found the disciples and told them, "I have seen the Lord!" Then she gave them his message.

JESUS APPEARS TO HIS DISCIPLES

[19] That Sunday evening the disciples were meeting behind locked doors because they were afraid of the Jewish leaders. Suddenly, Jesus was standing there among them! "Peace be with you," he said. [20] As he spoke, he showed them the wounds in his hands and his side. They were filled with joy when they saw the Lord! [21] Again he said, "Peace be with you. As the Father has sent me, so I am sending you." [22] Then he breathed on them and said, "Receive the Holy Spirit. [23] If you forgive anyone's sins, they are forgiven. If you do not forgive them, they are not forgiven."

JESUS APPEARS TO THOMAS

[24] One of the twelve disciples, Thomas (nicknamed the Twin), was not with the others when Jesus came. [25] They told him, "We have seen the Lord!" But he replied, "I won't believe it unless I see the nail wounds in his hands, put my fingers into them, and place my hand into the wound in his side." [26] Eight days later the disciples were together again, and this time Thomas was with them. The doors were locked; but suddenly, as before, Jesus was standing among them. "Peace be with you," he said. [27] Then he said to Thomas, "Put your finger here, and look at my hands. Put your hand into the wound in my side. Don't be faithless any longer. Believe!" [28] "My Lord and my God!" Thomas exclaimed. [29] Then Jesus told him, "You believe because you have seen me. Blessed are those who believe without seeing me."

PURPOSE OF THE BOOK

[30] The disciples saw Jesus do many other miraculous signs in addition to the ones recorded in this book. [31] But these are written so that you may continue to believe that Jesus is the Messiah, the Son of God, and that by believing in him you will have life by the power of his name.

21

EPILOGUE: JESUS APPEARS TO SEVEN DISCIPLES

[1] Later, Jesus appeared again to the disciples beside the Sea of Galilee. This is how it happened. [2] Several of the disciples were there—Simon Peter, Thomas (nicknamed the Twin), Nathanael from Cana in Galilee, the sons of Zebedee, and two other disciples. [3] Simon Peter said, "I'm going fishing." "We'll come, too," they all said. So they went out in the boat, but they caught nothing all night. [4] At dawn Jesus was standing on the beach, but the disciples couldn't see who he was. [5] He called out, "Fellows, have you caught any fish?" "No," they replied. [6] Then he said, "Throw out your net on the right-hand side of the boat, and you'll get some!" So they did, and they couldn't haul in the net because there were so many fish in it. [7] Then the disciple Jesus loved said to Peter, "It's the Lord!" When Simon Peter heard that it was the Lord, he put on his tunic (for he had stripped for work), jumped into the water, and headed to shore. [8] The others stayed with the boat and pulled the loaded net to the shore, for they were only about a hundred yards from shore. [9] When they got there, they found breakfast waiting for them—fish cooking over a charcoal fire, and some bread. [10] "Bring some of the fish you've just caught," Jesus said. [11] So Simon Peter went aboard and dragged the net to the shore. There were 153 large fish, and yet the net hadn't torn. [12] "Now come and have some breakfast!" Jesus said. None of the disciples dared to ask him, "Who are you?" They knew it was the Lord. [13] Then Jesus served them the bread and the fish. [14] This was the third time Jesus had appeared to his disciples since he had been raised from the dead. [15] After breakfast Jesus asked Simon Peter, "Simon son of John, do you love me more than these?" "Yes, Lord," Peter replied, "you know I love you." "Then feed my lambs," Jesus told him. [16] Jesus repeated the question: "Simon son of John, do you love me?" "Yes, Lord," Peter said, "you know I love you." "Then take care of my sheep," Jesus said. [17] A third time he asked him, "Simon son of John, do you love me?" Peter was hurt that Jesus asked the question a third time. He said, "Lord, you know everything. You know that I love you." Jesus said, "Then feed my sheep. [18] "I tell you the truth, when you were young, you were able to do as you liked; you dressed yourself and went wherever you wanted to go. But when you are old, you will stretch out your hands, and others will dress you and take you where you don't want to go." [19] Jesus said this to let him know by what kind of death he would glorify God. Then Jesus told him, "Follow me." [20] Peter turned around and saw behind them the disciple Jesus loved—the one who had leaned over to Jesus during supper and asked, "Lord, who will betray you?" [21] Peter asked Jesus, "What about him, Lord?" [22] Jesus replied, "If I want him to remain alive until I return, what is that to you? As for you, follow me." [23] So the rumor spread among the community of believers that this disciple wouldn't die. But that isn't what Jesus said at all. He only said, "If I want him to remain alive until I return, what is that to you?" [24] This disciple is the one who testifies to these events and has recorded them here. And we know that his account of these things is accurate. [25] Jesus also did many other things. If they were all written down, I suppose the whole world could not contain the books that would be written.

EPILOGUE: JESUS APPEARS TO SEVEN DISCIPLES

JOHN 21:1-13

READ

1. Read John 21:1-13 slowly (aloud, if it's not intrusive to others).
2. Look at the photo on pages 96-97.
3. Pause.

REFLECT

1. Read the text again, slowly.
2. Notice the enormous size of the rock formations in the photo. They could represent many things in the passage:
   - the presence of Christ, our rock
   - the powerful scene of great conversations such as Jesus and Peter's (see vv. 15-19)
   - Peter, the rock, eagerly rushing toward his friend even though he had betrayed his friend (v. 7)
3. Read the passage again and notice what the rock formations highlight for you.
4. Ask God why that might be.

5. Is there anything in this passage that resembles what you would like to experience with Jesus?
6. What, if anything, do you sense God inviting you to consider? To feel? To do?

RESPOND

1. Stand up tall, like the massive rock formations in the photo.
2. Place your hands on your hips.
3. Say (aloud, if possible) your response to God about what stood out to you.

REST

1. Rest in the words and images of this passage.
2. Exhale.
3. Soak in the ideas of Jesus who is practical (cooking breakfast), accompanying us in familiar places (the beach), befriending us as he did the disciples.

LIST OF GUIDED MEDITATIONS

CONTINUE THE CONVERSATION